MW01602902

Mary, Matrix of Change

Mary, Matrix of Change

Personal and Global Transformation
through the Rosary

Michele Maxwell

Illustrated by Amy Riggle

VANTAGE PRESS
New York

Published by Vantage Press, Inc.
419 Park Ave. South, New York, NY 10016

Manufactured in the United States of America
ISBN: 978-0-533-15957-4

Library of Congress Catalog Card No.: 2007909520

0 9 8 7 6 5 4 3 2 1

To the Kobernats

Contents

"Be transformed by the renewal of your mind."
—Romans 12:2

"It is a great glory and singular honor for us to have an origin so noble, an end so exalted, a center so divine . . . O my Sovereign End, my Divine Center, attract me, draw me completely to you, and do not allow me to oppose your power in any way!"
—St. John Eudes

"If I could only offer adequate thanks for such a great benefit as Mary! She is within me. What a precious possession and what a consolation for me."
—St. Louis de Montfort

"The whole life of Christ recapitulates itself ever anew in man."
—Monsignor Romano Guardini

"If Christ were born a thousand times in Bethlehem, but not in you, you would remain lost forever. . . . The Cross on Golgotha cannot redeem you from evil if it is not raised up also in you."
—Angelus Silesius

"The heart of spiritual courage is formed by a love of Truth. To say yes to Truth and to follow wherever it leads calls for the greatest courage. . . . There is no birthing more painful than this passage from shadows into the light, from the old man to the new. It is understandable that some lack the courage to submit to so penetrating a light."
—Servais Pinckaers, OP

Preface

The rosary can be prayed with benefit by any human being, of any religion or no religion, because it is about *being human*. It is about incarnation—life in a body. So if a person has been born of woman and taken on flesh, the rosary is for them. It is about the *evolutionary change*—the imperative of *transformation*—that alone gives meaning to bodily life on earth.

All creation, all truth, is multi-layered, and so are we. The integral approach is able to take in all levels of truth—both the historic Jesus and Mary of Palestine and the metaphysical Mary and Jesus that form our True and Absolute Self. In the search for the historic Jesus, we become so dazzled by the literal level of what happened in the Incarnation that we completely miss the other, deeper level of truth that it contains. This perennial, universal level of truth is found in all religions. Insofar as religions are dividers of humanity—Mary tells us in Medjugorje—they are not "real," but human constructs. Religions' true value lies in the *spiritual practice* they provide as uniters of humanity and all creation, drawing into One all incarnated beings on the evolutionary journey of spirit.

Mary's archetypal role as the True Self is always to point us toward Jesus the Christ, the Absolute Self, and say: "Do whatever he tells you." (*John 2:5*) In other words, live God's will, not the False Self's will. Transform from the False Self agenda of fears and desires and live as Mary, the True Self that is always conscious of the Absolute Self residing inside her womb—the presence of Christ within. Just as Mary's function in the Incarnation was to knit together the body and soul of Jesus the Christ, her role in our life is also to knit together body and soul throughout the course of our spiritual evolution. Her work is the work of *integration*. As a bridge, she joins human and divine in the depths of the Self, enabling them to function as one. The rosary is an integral spiritual practice that holds immense power and potential for bridging our human and divine natures, thus accelerating both personal and planetary evolution for the good of the world. I invite you to pick up the rosary and use it.

Mary, Matrix of Change

One

Medjugorje: Changing Lead into Gold

The Path of Evolutionary Spirituality

This year, 2009, is the 28th anniversary of the Marian apparitions in Medjugorje. In the summer of 1988, I spent one week in the village of Medjugorje, in the former Yugoslavia. It was still under Communist rule at the time. In that small village "between the hills" (as the name indicates), it was claimed that the Blessed Virgin Mary, the mother of Jesus, had been appearing daily since June 1981 to six children—Marija, Mirjana, Ivanka, Vicka, Ivan, and Jacov. The apparitions continue to this day, some 27 years later, but only to three of the six young people. All of the visionaries have grown up, married, and now raise families of their own. The Queen of Peace, as Mary identified herself in Medjugorje, remains.

I was not a Catholic when I went to Medjugorje, arriving there with a dubious, even skeptical, outlook on the alleged apparitions. Suffice it to say I was *changed* during my seven days there; humbled and silenced in my intellectual arrogance by a stunning series of supernatural events that I could not possibly explain. "With prayer even the laws of nature can be suspended," Mary had claimed there. And I saw evidence of that, again and

1

again, both alone and in large groups of pilgrims who witnessed "miracles" en masse. I found that Medjugorje, while thoroughly Catholic, was drawing people of all nations and cultures, of all religions and no religion. The recurring theme of Mary's messages was simple: *"Pray, pray, pray."* And the stated goal of prayer was also simple: *"Conversion of heart."* Not conversion to Catholicism, or to any particular church. In one of Mary's messages in Medjugorje, she said that for God there are no such divisions as Muslim, Jew, and Christian; those divisions are made by us, not God. From the perspective of heaven, she said, all human beings are equally and simply children of God . . . and children of Mary.

One of the most common phenomenal signs that occurs in Medjugorje forms the basis of this book. In Medjugorje, the rosary is prayed incessantly: by pilgrims riding the bus and walking the red dirt pathways that crisscross the vineyards, by villagers as they go about their daily work or climb barefoot at dusk to the rocky top of Apparition Hill (Mt. Podbrdo), by the whole community before and after Mass at St. James Church each evening, with people spilling out of the sanctuary onto the plaza outside. The rosary is prayed as people wait in line to go to Confession—the Sacrament of Reconciliation—and as they make the arduous ascent to the top of Cross Mountain (Mt. Krizevec), where a huge concrete cross was erected by the villagers in 1933 to commemorate 1900 years of local faith in the Crucified One. The rosary is prayed by Sr. Elvira's community of recovering drug addicts and by those who sit in the silent adoration chapel before the Blessed Sacrament, by youth groups on retreat from all over the world, and by hordes of white-haired retirees. The rosary seems somehow foundational to Medjugorje.

The "phenomenon"—as if there is anything more phenomenal than this incessant praying of the rosary—is that in Medjugorje, people's rosaries change *from lead to gold.* This means that there is a dramatic visible conversion of the chain or beads upon which one prays, from silver-colored lead to a burnished yellow gold. It doesn't happen to everyone, but it is a very common occurrence. It happened to me—a non-Catholic, non-rosary praying skeptic—before I even began to use the rosary (given to me by a Catholic friend) that I had hastily stashed in my backpack before leaving the U.S. A few hours after my arrival in Medjugorje, when I realized that the rosary was an obsession of the place, I decided to pull mine out. Somewhere between Texas and Medjugorje, my rosary had changed from silver-toned metal links and chain into *gold.* This dramatic and inexplicable transformation set the tone for all that followed. I had entered into the matrix of conversion that is Mary. I had entered into her divine alchemy and the consuming fire where lead is transformed into gold. The *change* is the thing.

Spiritually, gold is the symbol of the transformed state and lead is the raw material. What happens when lead becomes gold? Spiritually speaking, this is a process of transformation in which the ego structure burns, dematerializes itself, and then merges with the whole. From there a new self emerges, the Authentic "I" based on immersion in the whole—a Real Self that is the product of cosmic knowledge. This transformation from lead to gold—from an ego-based life into a True Self-based life—begins a process of *ongoing evolution.* Conversion is daily and ongoing, with no fixed endpoint. This evolutionary transformation or *change* is the heart of the spiritual journey: the *continual rising in consciousness levels.* The "conversion of heart" Mary requires in

3

Medjugorje is the journey of transformation from a life lived at the level of the ego or False Self, enslaved to the narcissistic desires and fears of one's emotional programs for happiness (as Fr. Thomas Keating calls them), to a life lived at the level of the True Self, the Authentic Self, or the Real "I." From that level of freedom, we are called to move still further, into participation in the Absolute Self, the Divine Nature that indwells us and all of creation. And so the Medjugorje sign of the rosary turning gold is a physical symbol of this *law of the transmutation of one nature into another* that lies at the heart of the spiritual journey and forms the meaning of human life.

In the years since that first trip to Medjugorje, I have come to see that the rosary is not only a sign or symbol but also an *instrument* of this conversion of heart, this transmutation of nature, this transformation of consciousness. It operates on multiple levels; on the conscious level of prayer that is wakeful and intentional, but also on the unconscious level of simply holding the beads in one's hands or gazing at a rosary mandala in silent, nonconceptual meditation. The rosary itself is "full of grace"!

In the Incarnation, Mary, the matrix of conversion, is the bridge between earth and heaven. Her goal now, as always, is to lead people to Jesus, to the Indwelling Christ that is the Absolute Self of every human being. For "through him all things were made." (*Col. 1:16*) Thus, every person is a sacred vessel of Divine Indwelling. Mary's goal is the enabling of each person's Absolute Self, the Indwelling Christ or "I AM" presence, to have direct contact with their earthly, bodily existence. This was her role in the Incarnation of Christ her son, and it is still her role today, with each one of us. Mary is the bridge that unites and integrates the Divine Christ of our Absolute Self with the world of form in which we live. She is the matrix of conversion, of our human transformation wherein the "I AM" or Absolute Self gradually becomes *integral to* and *incarnate in* all that we think, say, feel, and do. Mary is the bridge of alignment, aligning our heart's desire with the will of God, so that her command to "Do whatever he tells you" is thoroughly integrated within us, from moment to moment.

By praying the rosary, we are contacting the deep mysteries of our own existence, many of which lie outside of our conscious awareness. While the structure of the rosary in its twenty mysteries revolves around the life of Mary and Jesus, in fact it represents the movement of each human being through the spiritual journey of evolving consciousness that is being recapitulated in these scenes from the journey of the Christ. Jesus and Mary together are, for those who pray the rosary, "everyman" and "everywoman." And even more intimately than that, they are archetypal symbols of the Inner Being of each and every individual person in the world. Looking at it from this point of view, Mary is an archetype of the True Self, Authentic Self, or Real "I" of each person. Jesus risen is the Christic Self, the Divine Indwelling, "Immanuel-God-with-us," or Self Absolute of each person. Only the True Self (Mary) can bring forth into Incarnation the Absolute Self (Christ). The False Self or ego-based self knows nothing of the Divine Indwelling and has no way to contact it. The "Mary" level of consciousness—the Real "I" or True Self—is full of grace, aware of the Divine Indwelling, completely in touch with the Inner Christ, and thus yielded or surrendered, joyfully, to the will of the Absolute Self (God), from moment to moment. Thus "Mary"—our True Self—is the bridge between the "earth" of our ego and the "heaven" of our Absolute Christ-self, which is Indwelling Divinity.

When Mary, Queen of Peace, in Medjugorje pleads for "conversion of heart" and rosaries change from lead to gold, *this* is the change that is being taught: the law of the transmutation of one nature into another—the transformation and transubstantiation of *evolutionary consciousness* that takes us from the merely human, ego-driven personal self to the divinely-human Integrated or Christic Self. We experience this conversion by crossing the bridge of Mary: the True Self. The rosary is completely at the service of this project, and one of the most effective spiritual practices for accomplishing it.

Two

Prayer Beads through the Ages

When we pick up the rosary, we are joining a long and venerable tradition of spiritual practice that spans cultures, religions, and epochs of history. Archeologists have found evidence of prayer beads used as early as 40,000 years ago. Praying on beads has always been viewed as a powerful tool of spiritual transformation. The string of beads is an outward reminder of our inner spiritual space, of something sacred about our self, an aspect that will never die, our eternal soul. It is a tool for *remembering,* for *recollection,* that summons us to inner peace. The word "bead" comes from the Old English word "bede" meaning "prayer," and is related to the ancient Sanskrit word "bodh" meaning "awakening" or "enlightenment" (as in the Buddha).

From ancient times, the bead has been recognized as an object of special relationship to the spiritual world—whether made of seeds, nuts, shells, bones, wood, gemstones, or glass. It is seen as a mysterious link between the seen and unseen worlds. The relationship between prayer and prayer beads is ancient and mystical. Beads are a physical, tangible reminder of the intimacy of the Divine indwelling our self and the events of our life. The deep symbolism of prayer beads is that they reflect the many incidents of our life—the sufferings, pains, joys, sorrows, and everyday events—while the thread or string of our *soul* is running through everything, a connecting link, holding everything together in a unified circle, giving shape and meaning to the "beads" or events of life. It is the chain or rope going through the beads that holds it all together. Perhaps this is why in Medjugorje, it is the rosary chain, representing the deepest, most authentic core of the self, that turns gold. Like the prayer on beads, our life journey rotates around and around a circle, with all things integrated by the indwelling spirit of God.

The oldest known tradition of prayer beads is *Hindu,* beginning 8,000 years ago in India with the "mala" or rose garland with its 108 beads to represent 108 earthly desires that must be transcended, or the 108 sacred names for the Ganges River. It is usually sandalwood scented. *Buddhist* prayer beads also originated in India, with the same number of beads as the Hindu. On each bead the Buddhist chants the mantra, "Om Mani Padme Om!" ("The Jewel is in the lotus.")

Islamic or *Muslim* prayer beads are called "zikr," "tasbih" or "subha" beads, a string of 33 beads prayed three times, on which one recites the 99 names of God or Allah. It is a God-praising instrument, adopted from India in the 9th century. In *Judaism*, the "talith" or prayer shawl is similar to prayer beads. Made of blue and white silk, with four tassels, eight strings, five knots, and six hundred fringes, it is a reminder of the 613 mitzvot or commandments. It was commanded to be used in Mosaic law (Deuteronomy 22:12 and Numbers 15:37), meant to form a "tent" for prayer and a Torah environment in which the holiness of life is remembered.

In the Christian *Eastern Orthodox* tradition, the "chotki"—a black woolen prayer rope with knots—is prayed continuously. On each knot one prays the "Jesus prayer"—"Lord Jesus Christ, Son of God, have mercy on me a sinner" (from Luke 18:9, the prayer of the publican). This practice goes back to the 7th century "prayer of the heart," where the tassel was designed to "dry one's tears." It was made famous in the 19th century classic book, *The Way of the Pilgrim,* about a Russian Orthodox pilgrim instructed by an old monk to pray the Jesus Prayer 3,000 times a day. A chotki with 30 knots would thus be prayed 100 times.

The **Roman Catholic Christian** rosary of the Blessed Virgin Mary had its origins in the Middle Ages. Popular Catholic lore attributes it to St. Dominic who received it directly from Mary in a vision. Additionally, we know of its gradual development in the "Paternoster Guilds" of medieval Europe and as a way for lay people without Bibles to somehow enter into the spiritual practice of religious orders which daily prayed the 150 Psalms. Since there were originally fifteen decades of the rosary—150 Hail Mary's—it was known as "Our Lady's Psalter," a prayer of and for ordinary people.

Throughout this long and varied history of prayer beads used across many cultures and religions of antiquity, there has been a common spiritual experience and realization about their use. Whether Hindu, Buddhist, Muslim, Jewish, or Christian, the practice is designed to move one *out of the head and into the heart,* or core being—to aid in connecting with the sacred presence of God within. In all the traditions, *repetitive prayer of a short sacred phrase or word* helps to silence the mind, empty one of excesses, simplify and make one less complicated and fragmented, more grounded, more in balance and harmony, more aware and awake, less reactionary, angry and defensive, and more loving. All peoples throughout history have found a similar experience in the

9

use of prayer beads to help with recollection, sensing the nearness of God, detachment from problems, and greater freedom within our human condition.

Three

The Prayers on the Beads

The rosary is a circle of beads consisting of five "decades" or sets of ten, separated by a single bead between each decade. On the single beads we pray the "Our Father" or "Lord's Prayer," taken from Matthew 6:9-13 and Luke 11:2-4. On the decade beads, ten at a time, we pray the "Hail Mary," taken from Luke 1:28, 42. Thus the bead prayers are entirely scriptural. In addition to these, the *Apostle's Creed* is prayed at the beginning of the rosary, the *"Glory Be"* doxology is prayed at the end of each decade, and the *"Hail Holy Queen"* (Salve Regina) is prayed at the conclusion of the rosary. (See Appendix.) These are ancient Marian and Trinitarian prayers of the Church, inspired by scripture but not direct biblical quotes, as are the "bead prayers."

Each decade of Hail Mary's represents one "Mystery" that is being contemplated, and all five decades (one full circle around the rosary's fifty beads) constitutes a praying of one "Set of Mysteries." Traditionally, a complete rosary consisted of three sets of mysteries—the *Joyful, Sorrowful,* and *Glorious*—five decades each or fifteen decades total, meaning three times around the circle of fifty beads. But in 2001, after some 500 years of the rosary's traditional 15-decade, 3-Mystery format, Pope John Paul II added a fourth set of mysteries—the *"Lumi-*

nous" mysteries—to this ancient prayer form. So now the complete rosary consists of twenty decades or four turns around the circle of five decades, and we now have five new "Mysteries of Light" to contemplate as we pray. Thank you, John Paul II! It is customary for Catholics to pray one set of mysteries each day, since one trip around the circle of beads takes 15–20 minutes, the maximum amount of time that most people can afford. So on Mondays and Saturdays it is customary to pray the Joyful Mysteries; on Tuesdays and Fridays the Sorrowful Mysteries; on Wednesdays and Sundays the Glorious Mysteries; and on Thursdays the Luminous Mysteries.

Let us now take a closer look at the two "bead prayers" that dominate the rosary: the "Our Father" and the "Hail Mary." While the Lord's Prayer or Our Father is the best-known prayer among Christians across all denominations, few of us have ever experienced a translation of this prayer of Jesus taken directly from his native Aramaic language in which it was taught. Instead, we have inherited, in our various Christian communions, translations that have passed from Aramaic to Greek to Latin to English. What has been lost in translation is any real sense of the original Hebrew dialect that was Jesus' native tongue. In the Aramaic language, for example, the word that has been rendered in English "Father" is actually without gender, and has a broader meaning, such as "birther" or "Father-Mother." Ancient Aramaic language recognized many levels of meaning and every word had many different meanings. Thus there could be many different versions of the Lord's Prayer, all based on the original ancient Aramaic. Here is an English translation by Neil Douglas-Klotz from *Prayers of the Cosmos,* taken directly from the Aramaic.

O Birther! Father-Mother of the Cosmos
Focus your light within us—make it useful.
Create your reign of unity now—
Through our fiery hearts and willing hands
Help us love beyond our ideals
And sprout acts of compassion for all creatures.
Animate the earth within us: we then
feel the Wisdom underneath supporting all.
Untangle the knots within
so that we can mend our hearts' simple ties to each other.
Don't let surface things delude us,
But free us from what holds us back from our true
    purpose.

Here is another English translation taken directly from the Aramaic, a Nazarene transliteration:

O Cosmic Birther, from whom the breath of life comes,
Who fills all realms of sound, light and vibration.
May Your light be experienced in my utmost holiest.
Your Heavenly Domain approaches.
Let Your will come true in the universe just as on earth.
Give us wisdom for our daily need,
Detach the fetters of faults that bind us,
Like we let go the guilt of others.
Let us not be lost in superficial things,
but let us be freed from that which keeps us
off from our true purpose.

These versions of the Lord's Prayer have translated the ancient Aramaic words of Jesus with a broader, more all-encompassing sweep of the various possible meanings that the original language carried for each individual word of the prayer. They are thus more comprehensive, less circumscribed and edited versions than our English translations which have passed through Greek and Latin to get to us.

Below is the traditional English translation used in the rosary. Note that the common concluding doxology used by many Christians, *"For thine is the kingdom, and the power, and the glory, forever and ever, Amen"*—a liturgical addition of the early Church not present in the scriptural version of the prayer—is not used in the rosary.

Our Father who art in heaven,
Hallowed be Thy name.
Thy kingdom come. Thy will be done
on earth as it is in heaven.
Give us this day our daily bread,
and forgive us our trespasses as we forgive
those who trespass against us.
And lead us not into temptation,
but deliver us from evil.

It has been noted by scholars that the Lord's Prayer seems to borrow heavily from the Hebrew Kaddish in the Talmud, and in fact may be constructed, especially in the first three sentences, almost verbatim from that traditional Jewish prayer that Jesus would have surely known. The fundamental truth of the prayer is the Law of Correspondence: *"As above, so below."* There is an assertion that earth must mirror heaven, the physical reflect the spiritual. The key correspondence between the Divine will and the human will is to be manifested in the *forgiveness of sins,* a unique means by which evolution of consciousness can accelerate. Reverence, submission, and humility are to characterize our human stance toward God who is the Source for all potential correspondence we can achieve between "above" and "below." This prayer stands at the entryway into each of the mysteries of the rosary as an affirmation of our purpose: perfect correspondence between our own mind and the mind of God, and deliverance from the temptations to evil of the False Self.

Now let us turn to the prayer that makes up the bulk of the rosary: the Hail Mary, repeated some 200 times if one prays the entire four sets of mysteries, or twenty decades at one sitting. In Medjugorje, Mary's constant refrain has been, "*Pray, pray, pray!*" Through her "School of Prayer" there, what have we learned about the meaning of prayer? How does prayer affect our evolution of consciousness? Much of it is summed up in the Hail Mary:

Hail Mary, full of grace,
the Lord is with you.
Blessed are you among women
and blessed is the fruit of your womb, Jesus.
Holy, Mary, Mother of God,
pray for us sinners now and at the hour of our
death. Amen.

The Hail Mary is essentially a Bible quote, drawn from two famous scenes: the scene of the *Annunciation* when the Angel Gabriel greets Mary—"Hail, full of grace! The Lord is with you." (Luke 1:28); and the scene of the *Visitation* of Mary to Elizabeth, when the unborn John the Baptist leapt in his mother's womb, causing Elizabeth to exclaim: "Most blessed are you among women, and blessed is the fruit of your womb." (Luke 1:42) For many years these two scriptural quotes constituted the entire Hail Mary prayer. Later the third sentence was added: "Holy, Mary, Mother of God, pray for us sinners now and at the hour of our death," thus making the prayer an explicit supplication to Mary.

It would be hard to find a more humble and simple prayer than the Hail Mary, and its utter simplicity and humility hold the key to its greatness as a tool for conquering the ego. Some people find the Hail Mary's repetition of *"Pray for us sinners"* a distasteful self-judgment. Yet it should be noted that in the original Hebrew language of this Jewish mother who calls us to pray, the word for "to pray"—*"l'hitpallel"* —means to *judge oneself.* Recall that in the Gospel parable of the two men who went to pray in Luke 18:9, their "prayer" was essentially a self-evaluation—one speaking from the egoic or False Self level of consciousness, the other from the True Self, giving rise to the "Jesus Prayer": *"Lord, have mercy on me, a sinner!"* Contemplative or meditative prayer in the Christian tradition is inevitably an opening to Reality, an awakening to one's true state, both positive and negative.

As we say "Hail, Mary," we spiritually reach out from our egoic level to our own True Self, acknowledging her as "full of grace," truly the Mother of the Lord within us who is the "fruit of her womb." We should whisper to our True Self a thousand times a day, *"The Lord is with you!"* This awareness of the indwelling Presence of God at our deepest core is the most crucial realization we can have on the spiritual journey, for the False Self system with its myriad insecurities and foibles is born of the ignorance of this fact. It will be dismantled only through an awakening to the Divine Indwelling that Gabriel announced to the Blessed Virgin. *"Blessed are you,"* and *"Blessed is your fruit"* are vital insights, as well. To be a human infused with divinity is an unparalleled and unending blessing for which we should be grateful at all times. Prayer awakens us to this ultimate reality of our **blessedness.**

When we ask our True Self, Mary, to "pray for us sinners now and at the hour of our death," we are humbly admitting that our ordinary, False Self level of consciousness is the origin of our "sin" and therefore must die and ultimately reach the "hour of death" when the ego burns up in the consuming fire of Love that is the Absolute Self. We ask for the maternal pity and compassion of our True Self upon the limited and sinful nature of our False Self heading toward inevitable death. We plead for our True Self to intercede and escort our False Self, lovingly, to its demise by drawing us into an ever-greater awareness of the Self Absolute indwelling our inmost being—Christ, whom we join by crossing the bridge of integration that is Mary.

Four

Getting the Rosary "Outside the Box": The New Cosmology

At this point it is important to say that all religions, including Christianity, have an outer or exoteric dimension, and an inner or esoteric dimension to their teachings. In approaching the rosary as an instrument of conversion á la Medjugorje, we are dealing with the *inner* dimension of Christianity. Mary, Queen of Peace in Medjugorje is calling us to something much deeper than the ordinary "mythic membership" level of belief in Church dogmas or the passive regurgitation of Bible stories and catechism doctrine. She is calling us to radical ***transformation of consciousness*** through serious spiritual practice. This challenges us not only to think outside the box, but ***pray*** outside the box.

This is not to say that we are throwing away the box! In evolution of consciousness there is a gradual, ongoing integration of truth at every level, so that we are always in the process of ***transcending and including.*** This means that, as we look at the mysteries of the rosary which comprise the major tenets of Christian faith, we are able to acknowledge the multiple levels of truth and meaning they embody. In announcing the mysteries we pray, we can say that Jesus was conceived of a Virgin by the Holy Spirit, was born, performed miracles, taught, got crucified, died, resurrected, and ascended—all of this on a literal, historical level. Yet we can also see *through* all of these dogmatic statements to levels of mystery and meaning that transcend the literal-historical aspect. We can both transcend and include the literal dogmatic level of belief, no longer identifying exclusively with it as the totality of the Christian message, but using it as a springboard into the deeper mystery of the *Christ-life pattern* that each one of us lives on this earth. In doing so, we do not denigrate, dilute, discard, or discount any of the dogmatic formulas of the Church's creed; we include them in love and compassion while also transcending them by looking "through" them to the deeper, hidden, more esoteric truths they contain.

To "transcend" our belief in the Virgin birth of Jesus is not to annihilate or discard it, but to include it as a teaching in service to, and as an expression of, an even deeper truth. In this book, we will be looking "through" each mystery of the rosary, including its literal meaning while transcending it in the service of conversion of heart or transformation of consciousness: Mary's alchemy of turning lead to gold. This, in fact, is the secret of the rosary's power to change: each set of mysteries progressively transcends and includes the preceding "lower" level. All levels—Joyful, Sorrowful, Luminous, Glorious—are honored for the truth they contain, even as we cease to identify exclusively with each one's truth, and move, as up a spiral staircase, into an integration of all Truth as One. This is why the rosary finds its "level" in each person who prays, like water finding its level in whatever container it is poured into. The rosary is equally adaptable and effective in a child, a teenager, an adult, an old person—and at whatever level of theological understanding or development of consciousness a person might have reached, or whatever level of spiritual maturity.

How are we to understand this mysterious adaptability of the rosary to diverse levels of awareness? The insights of what is called the "New Cosmology" are helpful here. The rosary first appeared in the Middle Ages, and, like all medieval spirituality, it carried the sensibilities and presuppositions of the dominant worldview of its time. The universe was understood to be hierarchical, with God an external force, separate from creation, imposing form on matter from outside. This medieval cosmology has been shattered by quantum physics, astronomy, and other scientific breakthroughs of the past few centuries, which have yielded a much richer view of the universe than what was accessible to medieval philosophers and theologians. This is the "New Cosmology" or "New Universe Story." (*Brian Swimme*)

St. Thomas Aquinas, the preeminent medieval theologian who penned the foundational theology of the Roman Catholic Church, wrote: "A mistake about the universe is a mistake about God." Therefore a new Universe Story calls for a new God-Story; a new cosmology calls for a new theology. The rosary is uniquely suited for this transition and capable of adaptation to the emerging truths of our universe. Here are a few of the key insights of the New Cosmology:

1. **The Universe Is an Expanding, Emerging Process.** It operates by "creative emergence" and endless generosity. Everything is evolving, expanding, emerging, becoming more itself—from the microscopic, cellular, atomic level to the planetary, stellar, galactic, universal, cosmic level. This expansion is infinite. Our job as human beings is to interact with all Creation in a mutually en-

hancing, sustainable way as we, too, embody this emerging process in our own lives. (*Brian Swimme*)

2. **The Universe Is Holistic.** Each part is a "holon" or dimension, mode and microcosm of the whole. Each part contains and operates by the same cosmic principles as the whole. The ancient metaphysical expression of this truth is: "*As above, so below.*" This holistic universe is omni-centric, each part being a "centration point" of the whole, with the universe organizing itself around each part as the "center." Each person, each being, is a small universe, a world in miniature. All form an interconnected whole. As St. Paul said, "You are Christ's body and individually parts of it." (*1 Cor. 12:27*)

These first two insights of the New Cosmology—the universe as both omni-centric and infinitely expanding—are summarized in the ancient, pre-scientific axiom quoted by St. Augustine and many medieval thinkers: "*God is a circle whose center is everywhere and whose circumference is nowhere.*"

3. **The Universe Is Grounded in a "Quantum Vacuum" of Absolute Nothingness.** Everything emerged from this "all-nourishing Abyss" of emptiness and space 13.7 billion years ago. This darkness of space is generative and is the ground of all creation; life emerges from it and returns to it. Therefore death is not a disaster but essential to the unfolding of the universe and its creative process of infinite expansion, evolution, and emergence. "Unless a grain of wheat falls to the ground and dies, it remains just a grain of wheat; but if it dies, it produces much fruit." (*John 12:24*) The human component of this process is a spiritual dying to the ego and the "self-emptying" ("*kenosis*") exemplified by Christ.

4. **The Universe Is Relational.** Matter emerges and manifests itself from within Creation through rela-

21

tionship—not from an outside force imposing form onto it. The power of relationship is "synergy," where 1+1=3; that is, something greater than the sum of its parts occurs when things combine and fuse. Only through tension, the relation of oppositional forces, does excellence emerge and evolution occur. Change happens through the mix of elements already in the stew, combining, relating, conflicting—not from an outside cook's hand imposing change.

5. **The Rule of the Emerging Universe Is Transformation, Conversion, Transmutation, Metamorphosis.** Change is ongoing, unending. In human experience, the price of change is death to the egoic self through detachment of the will. In religious language, this transformation is called divinization or deification, and it happens when we awaken to ourselves as the self-emptying "center" of the universe and manifest the powerful core nothingness that generates life. Our model for this is Jesus Christ crucified.

6. **The Universe Maintains Homeostasis,** stability in the midst of change. This is possible through a balance between random chaos and established rigidity. The perfect amount of chaos and randomness in creation is offset by cosmic forces of law and order. Both the artist and the judge, the whirling dervish and the Pope, the liberal and the conservative, are necessary to maintain a livable climate.

7. **The Universe Operates by the Law of Attraction.** Rocks and earth, protons and electrons, earth and sun, thought and deed, prayer and miracle—at every level of creation, there is allurement or attraction of energies that enables the universe to move forward, evolve, expand, emerge. Concrete events of reality, both positive

and negative, arise in response to energy (positive or negative) that <u>attracts</u> them.

8. **The Universe Reaches Its Ultimate Fulfillment "Now"—in the Present Moment.** Each moment is the climax of the Universe Story's unfolding, evolving process—until the next moment. To find and rest in the living center of each moment is to be truly conscious.

Following the holistic model of the new universe story, we will be viewing the mysteries of the rosary as mirrors of the cosmologic Big Picture; that is, seeing Mary and Jesus not only as separate persons, distinct from us in time and space, but as aspects, modes, dimensions, or holons of the One Body that we all share in Christ and therefore, <u>aspects of our very selves.</u> The milestones of the human-divine journey that comprise the twenty rosary mysteries are thus part of our own personal Universe Story, as well.

As we turn to the deep inner meaning of the rosary, let us see how each of the twenty Mysteries embodies the law of the transmutation of one nature into another. Let us see how each mystery moves one along the path of evolutionary consciousness and effects the principles of developmental change, from the pre-conscious and infantile stages of unaware/oblivious blessedness (Joyful), through the rigors of the False Self's pain-ridden programs and agendas (Sorrowful), toward enlightenment and realization of the True Self (Luminous), into the ongoing experience of the "Kingdom of Heaven" or the Absolute Self (Glorious). The Mysteries of the rosary lead us on the evolutionary journey of transforming the personal "I" with its purposes into the Absolute "I" with its purposes. This is the transformation from the dull, leaden gray of our merely human ego or False Self running the show, into the gold of the Divine-Human integration that is our True

23

Self: "I live, no longer I, but Christ lives in me." (*Galatians 2:20*)

In the following chapters, we will take a look at the mysteries of the rosary, seeking out the *evolutionary challenge* that is inherent in each of them as the spiritual journey proceeds in response to the changing conditions of life—the life of Jesus and Mary and of our life. Following each mystery's reflection, there is a suggested spiritual aim for that mystery; in this way we will bring the power of *conscious intention* and the universal *law of attraction* to bear on the praying of each decade.

Five

The Joyful Mysteries: Unconscious Divinity Awakening

First Joyful Mystery: The Annunciation

The angel Gabriel was sent from God to a city of Galilee named Nazareth, to a virgin betrothed to a man named Joseph . . . and the virgin's name was Mary. And coming to her, he said, "Hail, full of grace, the Lord is with you!" (Luke 1:26-28)

The True Self is always "a virgin betrothed." *Virginal* means empty and open. *Betrothed* means in love and committed—mind, body, and soul—to the Beloved. The Beloved is our Source, God-who-is-Love. Mary, as the True

Self, is "ever-virgin," a spacious, pure vessel, ever empty of ego and open to the Divine. Thus perpetual virginity is a hallmark of the True Self.

The Gospel tells us that Mary was frightened by the angel's words and did not understand what his greeting meant. There is here, as for all of us in the beginning of our journey, a *fear,* a *lack of insight,* an *ignorance* of God's power and design, and an *unconsciousness* of divinity standing at the threshold of our innermost being. As consciousness grows, fear dissolves.

Mary replies to Gabriel: *"Behold, I am the handmaid of the Lord. Let it be done to me according to your word."* This is the FIAT: saying YES to God's will despite confusion. The True Self is *empty and yielded* to the Absolute. It is the "hand-made" of the Lord, the very image of God, pottery from the potter's own wheel. *Openness of mind and heart* allows for the inbreaking of something *new,* the possibility of *change.* This is the vitally necessary pre-condition for change. Without openness of mind and heart, Gabriel could not have appeared or been heard by Mary. A pure and empty vessel is the Ground Zero of transformation.

What does this mean for us? God sends a message via "Gabriel" to the True Self ("Mary"), who is the *only one* through whom God will be able to physically manifest His presence in the real world. But the True Self, having free will, must respond with a "Yes" or "No" to the call of God. The False Self (personal self at the egoic level) will always say "No" to the Annunciation of inner divinity. This is because the ego can only see reality in the dualistic sense of subject and object, with all things separate, divided, and relative to each other. Having no apparatus with which to comprehend the eternal, limitless, unqualified One without a second—the Absolute Reality that Yahweh revealed to Moses as "*I AM*"—the ego cannot recognize inner divinity and thus cannot incarnate God. Only the True Self can; only our "Mary" can.

Suggested Prayer Intention for the 1st Joyful Mystery:

LET ME BE in my True Self a "virgin betrothed" ... both *virginal,* by an empty openness of mind and heart ... and *betrothed* in total commitment to my Source, God-who-is-Love. May my life be a continual "Yes" to the invitation of each moment to incarnate the Love within.

(If you wish, yoke this affirmation to a positive earthly intention; now pray the first decade.)

Second Joyful Mystery: The Visitation

In those days, Mary arose and went with haste into the hill country, to a city of Judah. ... And when Elizabeth heard the greeting of Mary, the babe leaped in her womb. "But who am I, that the mother of my Lord should come to me?" (Luke 1:39-41)

The True Self *goes with haste*. It rushes to share the Divine Indwelling with others, realizing that "now" is the time. The True Self, unlike the ego, does not delay or procrastinate but realizes the urgency of the (divinely) Present moment.

The True Self *exudes authority and presence*, evoking a response in others, just as Mary incited the womb-leaping exclamation of joy from her cousin Elizabeth. The True Self *humbles and awes* her listeners, just as Elizabeth was awed and humbled, saying, "Who am I, that the Mother of my Lord should come to me?" There is a *transparency* about Mary that enables others to "see through" to the Divine Indwelling at her center, the Christ within. The True Self reveals to the world the loving Source of life that is always present.

Mary replies to Elizabeth with her famous speech, the *Magnificat:* "My soul proclaims the greatness of the Lord; my spirit rejoices in God my savior. For he has looked upon his handmaid's lowliness; behold, all generations will call me blessed. The Mighty One has done great things for me, and holy is his name . . ." (Luke 1:46-55)

The True Self *magnifies the Absolute,* the Reality that is God, causing this Presence to grow larger through a life that is conscious. The True Self thus extols the grandeur, power, mercy, faithfulness, and eternity of God, drawing attention to the Divine Presence in all things. The True Self *gives attention* to Divinity and the love of God in *every person and situation,* rather than to the dark shadows of negativity or fear, thereby magnifying the energy of Love, Wisdom, Power, and Divine Light in the world. The True Self thus acts as a bridge between earth and heaven at all times.

Suggested Prayer Intention for the 2nd Joyful Mystery:

LET ME BE in my True Self *urgent and hasty* to bring to others the Divine Presence within me which awakens the Divine Presence in them, *magnifying* the Absolute Love-that-is-God in all that I think, say and do.

(If you wish, yoke this affirmation to a positive earthly intention; now pray the second decade.)

Third Joyful Mystery: The Birth of Jesus

And she gave birth to her first-born son and wrapped him in swaddling clothes, and laid him in a manger, because there was no place for them in the inn. (Luke 2:7)

The True Self brings forth Indwelling Divinity in *poverty*. The materialistic and consumeristic play no part in bringing forth the Christ Self, whose birth is character-ized by smallness, littleness, and humility. The True Self always tends toward *simplicity* rather than sophistica-tion or complexity. These are the values of the True Self, but because there is "no place for them" in the inn of domi-nant culture, it brings forth Indwelling Divinity amid great *hardship and inconvenience,* often in an environ-ment of adversity and cynical scorn. The world is gener-ally *inhospitable* to the emergence of the True Self, which is accompanied and comforted more appropriately by ani-mals and peasants. With the worldly far removed, the simple, humble and lowly are the greatest companions and nurturers of the True Self, midwifing the birth of the Indwelling Absolute Self. A living example of this is the fact that apparitions of the Blessed Virgin Mary have his-torically been to shepherds, illiterate peasants, and chil-dren—not to the wealthy or wise in the world's eyes.

Humility is the doorway to the True Self. The False Self or ego despises lowly, humble littleness, looking in-stead for grandeur, recognition, pomp and acclaim. At Christmas time and always, in thinking about the birth of Christ, let us remember the words of St. Augustine: "What does it avail me that this birth of Christ, the Son of God, is always happening if it does not happen in me? That it should happen in me is what matters." Just as the universe appeared out of the nothingness of a dark, empty abyss, so the Christ child entered the world in the humble obscurity of a rough feeding trough, and the Ab-solute Self of each person is manifested through the "handmaid's lowliness" of the True Self. Thus poverty coupled with conflict produces both physical and spiritual universes.

Suggested Prayer Intention for the 3rd Joyful Mystery:

LET ME BE in my True Self *displaced from easeful wealth,* bearing forth Divinity through its only possible channel: *simple humility.*

(If you wish, yoke this affirmation to a positive earthly intention; now pray the third decade.)

Fourth Joyful Mystery: Presentation of Jesus in the Temple

And when the parents brought in the child Jesus to perform the custom of the law in regard to him, Simeon took him up in his arms and blessed God . . . and said to Mary his mother, "Behold, this child is destined for the fall and rise of many in Israel, and to be a sign that will be contradicted (and you yourself a sword will pierce) so that the thoughts of many hearts may be revealed." (Luke 2:27-35)

The True Self seeks a spiritual *context* in which to frame life's experiences. Mary follows the Mosaic law,

31

takes Jesus to the Temple, and performs the purification rite for post-partum women. As bridge between earth and heaven, the True Self must cultivate more than isolated "spiritual experiences." Without a larger spiritual context to receive experiences, they fall on fallow ground and bear no fruit, being swallowed up in the onward march of life, washed out with the tide of everyday incidents. Or worse, they become fuel for the False Self, a feather in the cap of the ego that collects any experiences which might serve as trophies to its specialness and uniqueness. Spiritual context provides a daily *practice* that defeats the ego, for the ego has no use for a "regula" or rule of life to be followed. The False Self shuns community and context, for its constant message is that the self is alone, isolated, and separate from everything else in the world.

In the Presentation, Mary (the True Self) carries her extraordinary child into the *larger context* of the Jewish religion, and there encounters two elders—Simeon and Anna—who epitomize "spiritual context." They have spent their whole lives in *practice*: inhabiting the Temple, praying, fasting, and keeping vigil as they await the promised savior. They are agents of the homeostasis that keeps the universe in balance. As for Simeon's prediction that Jesus will be a sign of contradiction—the Absolute Self (Christ, God) will always be contradicted by the False Self (satan, ego). The world, dominated by satanic ego, will contradict Jesus; the False Self will bridle and buck against the Christ within. Mary will also be pierced by a sword, for the True Self will suffer a mortal blow as the bridge between earth and heaven, the agent of transmutation between the lead of the ego and the gold of the Absolute Self. When the True Self is "pierced by a sword," the secret thoughts of many are revealed—and there is room for all in the vast context that holds all opposites together in creative tension.

Suggested Prayer Intention for the 4th Joyful Mystery:

LET ME BE in my True Self immersed in the *context* of human and spiritual community so as to bear the contradictions of ego amid the "secret thoughts of many hearts"—not just my own.

(If you wish, yoke this affirmation to a positive earthly intention; now pray the fourth decade.)

Fifth Joyful Mystery: Finding the Child Jesus in the Temple

After three days they found him in the temple, sitting in the midst of the teachers, listening to them and asking them questions, and all who heard him were astounded at his understanding and his answers. When his parents saw him, they were astonished and his mother said to him, "Son, why have you done this

33

to us? Your father and I have been looking for you with great anxiety." And he said to them, "Why were you looking for me? Did you not know that I must be in my Father's house?" But they did not understand what he said to them. He went down with them to Nazareth, and was obedient to them; and his mother kept all these things in her heart. And Jesus advanced in wisdom and age and favor before God and man. (Luke 2:45-42)

In the scripture, this scene follows immediately upon the heels of the Presentation. On the cusp of an evolutionary step from one level to another, higher, level, the True Self undergoes *fear and anxiety,* the unnerving experience of *losing one's ground of being,* the inner Christ child who is the Absolute Self. In this dark hour before the Joyful Mysteries have given way to the Luminous ones in the movement from "I" to "we" consciousness, Mary is panic-stricken, distraught, astonished and uncomprehending of what Jesus has done. His response is a clear invitation to a higher level of consciousness, *transcending the purely personal stage of insulated comfort* in the nuclear family they have all known for twelve years, and the embarking upon a *quest for higher wisdom and union with God as the ruling passion of life*—more urgent, compelling and important than merely staying with the flock in the security of bodily and material contact. There is a dramatic *expansion* as the Absolute Self branches out, breaking the bonds of the in-house community and becoming immersed in the world of rabbinical study. We are told that Jesus "advanced in wisdom and age and favor before God and man." This is a clear statement of the *evolution of consciousness* that the Lord models for us as the normal course of our human development into divinization.

After the Temple episode, we are told that Mary "pondered all these things in her heart." The True Self emerges more and more as *a witnessing presence,* an interior observer of life's events that is unfettered by the fears and desires of the ego, free to look upon Reality as it is with the compassionate yet impartial eye of understanding.

Suggested Prayer Intention for the 5th Joyful Mystery:

LET ME BE in my True Self *expansive* beyond the boundaries of my comfort zone, stretching awareness of "me" into the loving commitment to "we" and pondering all things realistically, as a witnessing presence to my own life.

(If you wish, yoke this affirmation to a positive earthly intention; now pray the fifth decade.)

Six

The Sorrowful Mysteries: the Human Condition and Dying to Ego

First Sorrowful Mystery: The Agony in the Garden

Then Jesus came with them to a place called Geth-semane, and he said to his disciples, "Sit here while I go over there and pray." He took along Peter and the two sons of Zebedee, and began to feel sorrow and distress. Then he said to them, "My soul is sorrowful even to death. Remain here and keep watch with me." He advanced a little and fell prostrate in prayer, saying, "My Father, if it is possible, let this cup pass from me; yet not as I will, but as You will." When he returned to his disciples he found them asleep. He said to Peter, "So you could not keep watch with me for one hour? Watch and pray that you may not undergo the test. The spirit is willing, but the flesh is weak. . . . Behold, the hour is at hand when the Son of Man is to be handed over to sinners." (Matthew 26:36-45)

The egoic self lives in an *illusory world of isolation,* ever yearning for companionship but inevitably perceiving itself as cut off, alone, separated, in a state of existential loneliness, angst, and terror—betrayed by all supports toward which it looks for help. The human condition inevitably involves the frustration of expectations and the failure of desires and plans based on emotional programs for happiness that can never work—*programs for security, affection and esteem, power and control* (Fr. Thomas Keating). For a time we might have the illusion of gaining these, but ultimately they are a mirage that leaves the ego standing alone, without safety, without true love, without autonomy—revealed as delusional, null and void.

Agonizing is the realization that the cup of suffering is not ours to accept or reject, but something passed to us inexorably as part of our journey of evolving consciousness; *suffering* must be received as intrinsic to the death of ego. "The flesh is weak." The egoic, False Self is sorely tempted to flee from the cup of suffering required for transcendence, conversion, transformation. It is the Spirit within, the Self Absolute—through the cooperation of the True Self or Authentic "I"—that withstands the test of Gethsemane.

"*Stay awake and keep watch*" are two practical teachings of this mystery. Jesus asks of his disciples simple *awareness.* The oblivion of "sleep"—a retreat into low-level consciousness—is the enemy of spiritual evolution.

Suggested Prayer Intention for the 1st Sorrowful Mystery:

LET ME BE in my True Self *awake* and *aware, yielded in will* to the suffering necessary for transformation.

(If you wish, yoke this affirmation to a positive earthly intention; now pray the first decade.)

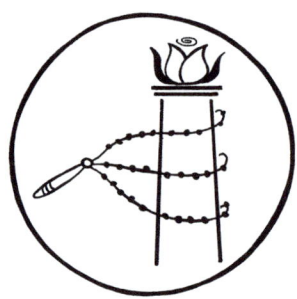

Second Sorrowful Mystery: The Scourging at the Pillar

Then Pilate released Barabbas to them, but after he had Jesus scourged, he handed him over to be crucified. (Matthew 27:26)

The ills that flesh is heir to, the physical pain and suffering that all humans experience as an inescapable fact of life in a body, owe their sting, above all, to the egoic or False Self. The ego scourges each person with the savage, brutal lashes of a flint-embellished whip, a knotted cord of furious strength unleashed on the human corpus. From the internal crawling frenzy of a heroin junkie to the seeping bed sores of a nursing home resident, from the tubercular wheeze and death rattle of a chain smoker to the diabetic amputations of a morbidly obese compulsive overeater, from the clogged arteries of a "Type A" overachiever to the poison-leaking botched implants of a beauty queen, from the myriad malignancies consuming the organs of cancer patients to the onslaught of viral infections from HIV, from a soldier's Agent Orange skin lesions and shrapnel-embedded spine to bulimic vomiting . . . our life in the physical body undergoes a scourging sooner or later.

Some physical ills are clearly traceable to one's own *False Self programs for happiness* that are doomed to failure; others the effects of *the collective ego* of a consumeristic, materialistic culture that gains financially from keeping both poor and rich in unhealthy lifestyles. Even the most health-conscious and responsible stewards of the body fall victim to the inescapable evils of unlabeled food additives, pesticide-ridden produce, and antibiotic-and-hormone-infused meat; land, air and water pollution, and other environmental toxins.

The True Self undergoes the scourging of the flesh in whatever form it takes—whether in chronic illness and disability or the sudden acute episodes of pain that punctuate life on earth. Nothing *humiliates* the ego as thoroughly as bodily disease, and therein lies its great spiritual potential for transformative power and fruitfulness.

There is always the possibility that the False Self will rise up in a rebellion of anger, resentment, and neurosis in the wake of physical suffering, as sometimes happens with embittered, negative, sour invalids. However, the potential for conversion of heart is also great, and many have testified to the effect, "I now thank God for my cancer (or other affliction) because through it I discovered my True Self and the Divine Presence within me."

Suggested Prayer Intention for the 2nd Sorrowful Mystery:

LET ME BE in my True Self *quickened and enlivened* through the scourging of my flesh as it blesses me with the humiliation of my ego.

(If you wish, yoke this affirmation to a positive earthly intention; now pray the second decade.)

Third Sorrowful Mystery: The Crowning with Thorns

Then the soldiers took Jesus inside the praetorium and gathered the whole cohort around him. They stripped off his clothes and threw a scarlet military cloak about him. Weaving a crown out of thorns, they placed it on his head, and a reed in his right hand. And kneeling before him, they mocked him, saying, "Hail, King of the Jews!" They spat upon him and took the reed and kept striking him on the head. . . . So Jesus came out, wearing the crown of thorns and the purple cloak. And Pilate said to them, "Behold, the man!" (Matthew 27:27–30; John 19:5)

The ego places on each person's head a crown of thorns. To journey the path of conversion from lead to gold, from the head to the heart, by far the most difficult passage is through the jungle of *thought* that is the overgrowth of the False Self. In this jungle we must all hack our way through *afflictive thoughts and emotions* of envy, jealousy, covetousness, pride, lust, greed, rage, fear, and guilt. The mockery of Jesus by the soldiers exemplifies this horrible psychological reality of the human condition.

Anger is a thorn that punctures our psychic scalp, sending searing pain and blood running into our eyes so that we "see red." Underneath the thorn of anger is the thorn of *fear* where thoughts of personal harm, neediness and lack haunt our imagination. What if we suffer (____)? What if we lose (____)? What if we never get (____)? The thorns of *envy* and *jealousy* are among the most brutal and damaging of all the afflictive thoughts that make up this crown of mental misery. Being consumed by what another person has or by the need to be held in a higher position of esteem and affection than someone else—such thoughts torment the mind in an endless circle of agony. *Lust* and *greed* are torturous twins, deceptive in their beginnings. While the attractions of the flesh and money start out in a challenging and exciting "thrill of the chase," both the desire for sexual pleasure and for the great almighty dollar lead to spiritual bankruptcy as their escalating obsessiveness begins to rule and enslave, sapping our inner freedom. And how those kissing cousins, *guilt* and *pride,* stab and bruise us with their sharp points! The moment that a thought of genuine contrition for a fault or mistake lingers too long in the mind, it becomes *guilt* and the moment guilt sinks its tentacles of self-accusation, condemnation and despair into our psyche, it becomes its mirror image: *pride*—the ego's calling card. For guilt is the flip side of arrogance, a deep shame and outrage that we have not behaved or appeared in a way that exhibits our true superiority and perfection. Our supremacy has been belied by our own actions, and guilt is the ego's rage and self-directed embarrassment at being caught out. True contrition looks nothing like guilt. It simply apologizes, makes reparation and moves on in humility, without fanfare, breast-beating or self-flagellation.

The human condition is one of *frequent mental distress* as our emotional programs for happiness, based on unrealistic, overblown needs for security, affection and control are constantly thwarted, thus triggering the afflictive emotions—thoughts charged with these frustrations that dominate our mind like a crown of thorns shoved roughly onto our head. The True Self stays afloat in this sea of the mind only by *prayer,* which counteracts negative thought. Throughout the mockery and crowning with thorns, Jesus must have prayed. In the face of our own bombardment of "monkey mind"—the million thoughts that drag us down each moment—Mary in Medjugorje says over and over: "*Pray, pray, pray!*" The practice of *meditation* has been the universal antidote to the crowning with thorns, across all the ages, cultures and religions of the world. Until each person begins to seriously work with *thoughts* the ego will continue to dominate consciousness and unleash a world of suffering.

Suggested Prayer Intention for the 3rd Sorrowful Mystery:

LET ME BE in my True Self free from the tyranny of every negative thought and afflictive emotion, quickly returning to my magnetic center through prayer.

(If you wish, yoke this affirmation to a positive earthly intention; now pray the third decade.)

Fourth Sorrowful Mystery: Carrying of the Cross

So they took Jesus, and carrying the cross himself he went out to what is called the Place of the Skull, in Hebrew, Golgotha. (John 18:16-17) As they led him away they took hold of a certain Simon, a Cyrenian, who was coming in from the country; and after laying

43

the cross on him, they made him carry it behind Jesus. (Luke 23:26)

Whoever wishes to come after me must deny himself, take up his cross, and follow me. For whoever wishes to save his life will lose it, but whoever loses his life for my sake and that of the gospel will save it. (Mark 8:34-35)

The False Self lays a cross on every person's shoulders, a burden of physical, emotional, mental and spiritual suffering to be carried by the True Self. Inevitably the narcissistic, egoic programs of the False Self will also affect other people, as our neuroses, obsessions, compulsions, and negative behavior must be borne by those around us. Our family—children, spouse, parents, siblings—and our friends and coworkers will be our "Simons," pressed into service to carry our cross behind us as we journey on the long and arduous way to ego death. The appearance of Simon in the gospels shows that we are communal creatures and our journey is never made alone; rather our lives are intertwined with other lives at every stage, whether we are aware of it or not.

In anticipation of his passion, Jesus taught his disciples that anyone who wishes to follow the Christic path of spiritual evolution must "deny himself, take up his cross, and follow me." To follow Christ on the Via Dolorosa to Calvary means that our spiritual evolution includes a conscious and deliberate renunciation of the False Self. This is "taking up" the cross with intention, rather than having it thrust upon us as victims of cruel fate. Jesus says, "I lay down my life in order to take it up again. No one takes it from me, but I lay it down on my own. I have power to lay it down, and power to take it up again." (*John 10:18*) We can say the same.

The power of the Absolute Self is the limitless power of God, the Divine Indwelling, the free life without end and without limits. To live this life, which is the birthright of every human being, begins with dying to the shadowy pseudo-life of the False Self. For many years this False Self with its afflictive emotions, painful illusions, and doomed programs for happiness must be "carried"—held in uncomfortable tension—by the True Self that is painfully aware of the "gap" between the falsehood and reality of the life one is living. In this long "in-between" time, victimization must come to an end with the acceptance of <u>responsibility</u> for whatever situation one has created. The ego clings to the noble victim role, hiding in blame and finger-pointing, projecting responsibility for one's sorry state outward, to parents or spouses or employers who abused their power and ruined one's life. In carrying the cross created by the False Self, walking toward its imminent execution and death, the True Self begins at last to participate in life in a meaningful way, no longer abdicating responsibility for present-day responses that are conditioned by past hurts and injustices.

Suggested Prayer Intention for the 4th Sorrowful Mystery:

LET ME BE in my True Self at all times intentionally laying down my life in the False Self, thus taking up the abundant life of the Absolute within by carrying my own cross responsibly.

(If you wish, yoke this affirmation to a positive earthly intention; now pray the fourth decade.)

Fifth Sorrowful Mystery: The Crucifixion

They brought him to the place of Golgotha (which is translated Place of the Skull). They gave him wine drugged with myrrh, but he did not take it. Then they crucified him and divided his garments by casting lots for them. It was nine o'clock in the morning when they crucified him. The inscription of the charge against him read, "The King of the Jews." With him they crucified two revolutionaries, one on his right and one on his left. Those passing by reviled him, shaking their heads and saying, "Aha! You who would destroy the temple and rebuild it in three days, save yourself by coming down from the cross." Likewise the chief priests, with the scribes, mocked him among themselves. . . . Those who were crucified with him also kept abusing him. At noon darkness came over the whole land until three in the afternoon. And at three o'clock Jesus cried out in a loud voice, "Eloi, Eloi, lama sabachthani?" which is translated, "My God, my God, why have you forsaken me?" . . . Jesus gave a loud cry and breathed his last. The veil of the

sanctuary was torn in two from top to bottom.
(Mark 15:22-38)

The mystery of the Crucifixion represents the most important rite of passage on the spiritual journey: the passing, in a definitive and absolute way, from a life lived at the egoic or False Self level of consciousness to a life lived at the "Mary" level or True Self state of being. Up until now, there have been experiences and even stages of False Self denial, where the ego has been conquered for brief periods, but this self-mastery has not become an abiding state of consciousness. Always there have been slips and slides back into the oblivion of narcissistic programs running on "automatic."

The final battle between the False Self and the True Self takes place in what classical Christian mysticism calls the "dark night of the soul." Essentially, it is a bloody mess, as the scourged body of Christ nailed to the cross so accurately depicts. At the intersection of the Cross's horizontal beam, where the ego holds sway over a miserable timeline of lives locked in past, present, and future slavery, and the vertical beam, where the True Self aligns with the Absolute Self in the upward thrust of Spirit into eternal bliss and freedom, a mighty conflict is held in tension. Certain things happen in this dark night at the Place of the Skull, the site of death. "For we who live are constantly being given up to death for the sake of Jesus, so that the life of Jesus may be manifested in our mortal flesh." (*II Cor. 4:11*)

Here is the blazing inferno into which the "lead" of our existence is tried and transformed into gold, with the lesser alloys of the False Self purged and burned away. It happens in many different ways: through tragic outward circumstances such as death, divorce, loss of loved ones,

47

drastic reversals of fortune, natural and manmade disasters, encounters with violence, war, crime; or through more interior means as a result of deep and prolonged meditation, introspection, or depression. However the "night" comes about, come it must for every soul, so that the lesser metals of the leaden False Self may be consumed in the fire of love that transforms one's life into an abiding consciousness at the level of the True Self.

Suggested Prayer Intention for the 5th Sorrowful Mystery:

LET ME BE in my True Self *abiding*, though the price be steep for this transformation of consciousness, which demands that my False Self be crucified completely, even unto death.

(If you wish, yoke this affirmation to a positive earthly intention; now pray the fifth decade.)

Seven

The Luminous Mysteries: Transformation and Life in the True Self

First Luminous Mystery: Baptism of Jesus

It happened in those days that Jesus came from Nazareth of Galilee and was baptized in the Jordan by John. On coming up out of the water, he saw the heavens being torn open and the Spirit, like a dove, descending upon him. And a voice came from the heavens, "You are my beloved Son; with you I am well pleased." At once the Spirit drove him out into the desert, and he remained in the desert for forty days, tempted by Satan. (Mark 1:9-13)

To be baptized is an act of humility. It is surrendering oneself into the hands of another person who submerges us beneath water, "burying" us, symbolically, along with the sins of our False Self, and then raising us up, symbolically, to a new life in the True Self that is "in Christ" (the Absolute Self). Upon rising from the baptismal water, we are clothed with the Holy Spirit, a fresh infusion of higher energy, power, and wisdom, a profound activation of the Spirit that has been present since our creation, but perhaps not part of our conscious awareness. Baptism is thus a symbolic re-enactment of the primordial evolutionary journey of human life from origins in the sea to emergence on land and the rising awareness of Spirit.

The first and foremost confidence bestowed by this Holy Spirit in baptism is the assurance that the True Self is the **beloved** of God, with whom God is "well pleased." We know ourselves, perhaps for the first time, as infinitely lovable and loved. The second confidence bestowed by the Holy Spirit is the *courage to confront the False Self* in its multiple manifestations—i.e. Satan in the desert. The egoic temptations to self-sufficiency and grandiosity constitute the demonic attack which Jesus eagerly faces after his baptism. Later, when Peter rebukes him for predicting his impending passion and ignominious death, Christ tells Peter, "Get behind me, Satan! You are thinking not as God does but as human beings do." (*Matthew 16:23*) The ego or False Self that drives such thought is the "Satan" we all must confront in order to restore the godliness of our full humanity.

Suggested Prayer Intention for the 1st Luminous Mystery:

LET ME BE in my True Self infused by the Holy Spirit with the conviction of being the Beloved of God, immensely pleasing in my very being, and eager to confront the demons in the desert of my False Self.

(If you wish, yoke this affirmation to a positive earthly intention; now pray the first decade.)

Second Luminous Mystery: The Wedding at Cana

On the third day there was a wedding in Cana in Galilee, and the mother of Jesus was there. Jesus and his disciples were also invited to the wedding. When the wine ran short, the mother of Jesus said to him, "They have no wine." Jesus said to her, "Woman, how does your concern affect me? My hour has not yet come." His mother said to the servers, "Do whatever he tells you." Now there were six stone water jars there for Jewish ceremonial washings, each holding twenty to thirty gallons. Jesus told them, "Fill the jars with water." So they filled them to the brim.

51

Then he told them, "Draw some out now and take it to the headwaiter." So they took it. And when the headwaiter tasted the water that had become wine, without knowing where it came from, the headwaiter called the bridegroom and said to him, "Everyone serves good wine first, and then when people have drunk freely, an inferior one; but you have kept the good wine until now." (John 2:1-10)

The True Self (Mary) is "there" when the mixed wine of our existence runs out, when need arises on any level—secular or sublime, spiritual or material, minor or catastrophic. The True Self calls upon the False Self to get onboard and bring relief. The ego will forever argue, "My hour has not yet come." I am too young, too old, too weak, too uneducated, too unskilled, too shy, too good, too prestigious, too clean, too dirty, too anything-and-everything—to help. But the True Self persists, saying, "Do whatever he tells you." DO whatever the Absolute Self at the core of being—the goodness of God within—is instructing. Do whatever the Holy Spirit infused at baptism is commanding you, is driving you to do. ***And do it now.*** The time is now, and only now. This present moment is the moment of decisive action. No more waiting, no more procrastination. Your hour *has* come. Seize the day, the hour, the moment, the second that is only real: now! Far from failing, when acting upon the True Self's injunction to heed the Absolute Self—Christ within—you will bring forth the choicest, superior, "good wine" of unimagined excellence.

The mystery of *transformation* is seen and tasted in the Cana experience: water becomes wine. Later, in the Eucharistic mystery, a drop of water, symbolic of our humanity baptized in the waters of divine grace, will be merged with a cup of wine to become the blood of Christ, nectar of divinity. The human and divine are merged in the one cup which we drink to our divinization. In the illumination of this spiritual passage, we experience within our own deepest interior the transformation of water into wine, of wine into blood, of lead into gold.

Suggested Prayer Intention for the 2nd Luminous Mystery:

LET ME BE in my True Self transformed from the limiting, narcissistic vision of the False Self into the sensitized awareness of need wherever it arises in the One Body of which I am a part. May I overcome all egoic lethargy and respond promptly to the needs of the present moment.

(If you wish, yoke this affirmation to a positive earthly intention; now pray the second decade.)

The Third Luminous Mystery: Proclamation of the Gospel

*After John had been arrested, Jesus came to Galilee proclaiming the gospel of God: "This is the time of fulfillment. The kingdom of God is at hand. Repent, and believe in the good news." (*Mark 1:14-15*)*

"Blessed are the poor in spirit, for theirs is the kingdom of heaven. Blessed are they who mourn, for they will be comforted. Blessed are the meek, for they will inherit the land. Blessed are they who hunger and thirst for righteousness, for they will be satisfied. Blessed are the merciful, for they will be shown mercy. Blessed are the clean of heart, for they will see God. Blessed are the peacemakers, for they will be called children of God. Blessed are they who are persecuted for the sake of righteousness, for theirs is the kingdom of heaven. Blessed are you when they insult you and persecute you and utter every kind of evil against you because of me. Rejoice and be glad, for your reward will be great in heaven!" (*Matthew 5:3-12*)

The Gospel or good news is bad news for the ego. The gospel perspective constitutes "enlightenment" or "illumination," and its light exposes clearly, once and for all, the dark shadows of the False Self. Christ's call to "*repent*" lies at the center of the gospel message. This call is a summons to conversion—to <u>change</u>. To repent is to "think again," to revise one's former goals and ambitions, to "change the direction in which one looks for happiness," as Fr. Thomas Keating describes it. Here begins in earnest the transformation from the "lead" of the ego to the "gold" of the True Self. Here, upon repenting and turning around, we begin at last to "get the lead out."

Repenting means that we are able to view our egoic programs for affection, esteem, power, control, and security with the luminosity of the Holy Spirit, shining a searchlight into the recesses of our motivations.

A brief survey of the Beatitudes reveals just how thoroughly the ego is routed out by repentance and conversion, and how radically new is the resulting state of consciousness. The values of the False Self are turned on their head in the gospel proclamation of the kingdom of God. While the ego strives for wealth, comfort, ease, diversion, power, control, satiety, vindication, vengeance, bodily pleasure, victory, accolades, praise, status, and flattery—all that belong to the sleek and the strong—the True Self's bliss lies in poverty, mourning, meekness, hunger and thirst for righteousness, mercy, cleanliness of heart, peacefulness, unjust persecution, and insults. All of the things that confound and humiliate the ego are blessings to the True Self—not because of a masochistic fetish for suffering, but because these things clear out the narcissistic clutter of mind and heart, creating the necessary *openness* for the Absolute Self to establish residency.

Suggested Prayer Intention for the 3rd Luminous Mystery:

LET ME BE in my True Self always repenting, thinking again, revising, changing, converting, and transforming, with open mind and heart, from an ego-centered life to a gospel life in Christ, the Absolute Self.

(If you wish, yoke this affirmation to a positive earthly intention; now pray the third decade.)

Fourth Luminous Mystery: The Transfiguration

Jesus took Peter, John, and James and went up the mountain to pray. While he was praying his face changed in appearance and his clothing became dazzling white. And behold, two men were conversing with him, Moses and Elijah, who appeared in glory and spoke of his exodus that he was going to accomplish in Jerusalem. Peter and his companions had been overcome by sleep, but becoming fully awake, they saw his glory and the two men standing with him. As they were about to part from him, Peter said to Jesus, "Master, it is good that we are here; let us make three tents, one for you, one for Moses, and one for Elijah." But he did not know what he was saying. While he was still speaking, a cloud came and cast a shadow over them, and they became frightened when they entered the cloud. Then from the cloud came a voice that said, "This is my chosen Son; listen to him." After the voice had spoken, Jesus was found alone. (Luke 9:28-36)

"While he was praying his face changed." The whole amazing experience of the Transfiguration which revealed Christ's "glory" happened "while Jesus was praying." We are changed, transfigured, transformed, and made transparent of glory through *prayer*. Like Peter, James, and John, the normal state of our egoic consciousness is one of being "overcome by sleep," but in prayer we become "fully awake" to the glory of the Absolute Self that indwells our inmost being. Moses and Elijah, symbolic of the Law and the Prophets, "converse" with the True Self in prayer, mediating to us the Love that sums up both, as Jesus taught: "You shall love the Lord, your God, with all your heart, with all your soul, and with all your mind. This is the greatest and the first commandment. The second is like it; You shall love your neighbor as yourself. ***The whole law and the prophets depend on these two commandments.*** *(Matthew 22:37–40)* The conversation that Moses and Elijah have with Jesus in prayer revolves around "the exodus he was going to accomplish in Jerusalem." This is the same exodus that each of us must accomplish through the collaboration of the True Self with the Absolute Self, ground-of-being, God-who-is-Love indwelling—that is, the crucifixion and death of the False Self that will liberate the True Self from the bondage and slavery of the ego's miserable tyranny.

That same ego will try to franchise even our spiritual gifts and the graces received in prayer, clinging possessively to any sensational experience that might bolster itself. The ego attaches to the mountaintop "peak experience": Let us build three tents here, stake our territory and move in permanently. The overshadowing cloud of divine Presence frightens the False Self's superficiality. Peter "did not know what he was saying," but "while he was still speaking" the cloud came down to swallow them up. And the voice from the cloud said, *"Listen to him."* **Stop talking and listen.** Shut up, Peter, and <u>listen</u>. Be quiet, egoic False Self, and <u>listen</u>. Transformation, transfiguring prayer is not the prayer of <u>words</u> born and spouted by the ego. Transfiguring prayer is listening rather than talking; it is silent. As Fr. Thomas Keating says, "God's first language is silence." Thus transfiguration of consciousness happens through meditation or contemplative prayer which grounds us in the empty, "All-Nurturing Abyss" of silent nothingness at the Source of creation.

Suggested Prayer Intention for the 4th Luminous Mystery:

LET ME BE in my True Self transfigured by *silent listening prayer,* so that my whole being reveals the glory of Christ, the Self Absolute who dwells within me.
(If you wish, yoke this affirmation to a positive earthly intention; now pray the fourth decade.)

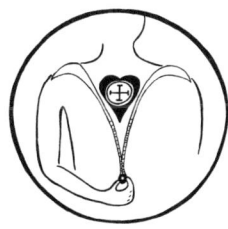

Fifth Luminous Mystery: The Last Supper—Institution of the Eucharist

While they were eating, Jesus took bread, said the blessing, broke it, and giving it to his disciples said, "Take and eat; this is my body." Then he took a cup, gave thanks, and gave it to them, saying, "Drink from it, all of you, for this is my blood of the covenant, which will be shed on behalf of many for the forgiveness of sins." (Matthew 26:26-28)

"Amen, amen, I say to you, unless you eat the flesh of the Son of Man and drink his blood, you do not have life within you. Whoever eats my flesh and drinks my blood has eternal life, and I will raise him on the last day. For my flesh is true food, and my blood is true drink. Whoever eats my flesh and drinks my blood remains in me and I in him . . . the one who feeds on me will have life because of me." (John 6:53-57)

The True Self is <u>embodied</u>, clothed with flesh and blood. The integral paradigm tells us that the <u>entire</u> person is divinized, including the ***body.*** Through evolution of consciousness—the gradual dismantling of the False Self so that the True Self (Mary) may bridge heaven and earth once more in each human life—we too may experience within our own being that in Christ (the Absolute Self), "the whole fullness of deity dwells *bodily.*" (*Colossians 2:9*) This is the Christian scandal: the scandal of an incarnate God. The Word made flesh means that every being in the world is to share in the Eucharistic mystery of becoming "one body, one spirit" with Christ. We are all *holons* of the *Whole* that is the Cosmic Christ "through whom all things were made, both visible and invisible." (*Colossians 1:16*) Therefore the True Self never attacks or devalues the human body. It is a heresy of the divisive ego that teaches that the body and soul are disconnected, that the body is a prison for the soul, that the body is base and evil while only the soul is pure and holy. These egoic heresies have had staggering consequences for human culture.

The transformation of bread and wine into the Body and Blood of Christ conveys the immense, unfathomable mystery of the ***integral oneness of all creation with God***—the Christic identity of each individual and the corporate identity of all humanity as one in Christ, simultaneously united, in our 14-billion-year-old stardust essence, with each other and with our Source.

Suggested Prayer Intention for the 5th Luminous Mystery:

LET ME BE in my True Self a walking tabernacle of the Eucharistic Presence of Christ, consuming the Body and Blood of unity with utmost consciousness of the Divine Indwelling that it quickens within me sacramentally, and sharing this Bread of Life with the world.

(If you wish, yoke this affirmation to a positive earthly intention; now pray the fifth decade.)

Eight

The Glorious Mysteries: Life in the Kingdom of God-Consciousness

First Glorious Mystery: The Resurrection

*When the sabbath was over, Mary Magdalene, Mary
the mother of James, and Salome bought spices so
that they might go and anoint him. Very early when
the sun had risen, on the first day of the week, they
came to the tomb. They were saying to one another,
"Who will roll back the stone for us from the entrance
to the tomb?" When they looked up, they saw that the
stone had been rolled back; it was very large. On en-
tering the tomb they saw a young man sitting on the
right side, clothed in a white robe, and they were ut-
terly amazed. He said to them, "Do not be amazed!
You seek Jesus of Nazareth, the crucified. He has*

been raised; he is not here. Behold the place where they laid him. . . . Then they went out and fled from the tomb, seized with trembling and bewilderment."
(Mark 16:1-8)

The resurrection of Jesus vividly portrays the dramatic inbreaking of the Kingdom to everyday human life. All bets are off. Anything can happen. The impossible has become possible, and evidently, nothing is impossible for God, just as Gabriel said at the Annunciation. The miraculous healings, exorcisms, feedings, and command of nature exhibited in Christ's ministry culminate in his triumph over death, bringing heaven to earth in fulfillment of his teaching: "The coming of the kingdom of God cannot be observed, and no one will announce, 'Look, here it is,' or 'There it is.' For behold, the kingdom of God is among [within] you." (*Luke 17:20–21*) This is why the angel tells the women at the empty tomb, "Do not be amazed!" Once the False Self has been dismantled and the True Self has risen, triumphantly united with the Self Absolute—the Indwelling Christ—the death-dealing perspective of limitation, scarcity, negativity, trepidation, and doubt is banished. The "impossible" is possible every day, for the Kingdom is within and among us. Potential and possibility are endless, and the evolutionary unfolding of consciousness is limitless. This is "the faith that saves" and moves mountains, so often praised by Jesus in those who were able to receive the miracles. "Nothing will be impossible for you," he promised. (*Matt 17:20*)

The Glorious Mysteries represent the radical inbreaking of a new level of consciousness that manifests in daily life as a huge evolutionary "leap," far surpassing the "mythic membership" level that comprises the majority of human consciousness today. In anticipation of such a radical shift, at Medjugorje, the "impossible" happens in nature regularly: silver turns to gold, the scent of roses bursts upon barren hilltops; the sun spins in a kaleidoscope of colors; crosses and fires appear and disappear; the terminally ill and permanently disabled are spontaneously healed and restored to health. And everywhere, as background music to the impossible, the rosary is prayed.

Suggested Prayer Intention for the 1st Glorious Mystery:

LET ME BE in my True Self resurrected each morning from the tomb of the False Self with its death-dealing fears, needs and insecurities. May the Risen Christ, my Self Absolute, triumph now through the consciousness of infinite possibility.

(If you wish, yoke this affirmation to a positive earthly intention; now pray the first decade.)

Second Glorious Mystery: The Ascension

He presented himself alive to them by many proofs after he had suffered, appearing to them during forty days and speaking about the kingdom of God. . . . When they had gathered together they asked him, "Lord, are you at this time going to restore the kingdom to Israel?" He answered them, "It is not for you to know the times or seasons that the Father has established by his own authority. But you will receive power when the Holy Spirit comes upon you, and you will be my witnesses in Jerusalem, throughout Judea and Samaria, and to the ends of the earth." When he had said this, as they were looking on, he was lifted up, and a cloud took him from their sight. While they were looking intently at the sky as he was going, suddenly two men dressed in white garments stood beside them. They said, "Men of Galilee, why are you standing there looking at the sky? This Jesus who has been taken up from you into heaven will return in the same way as you have seen him going into heaven." Then they returned to Jerusalem from the mount called Olivet. (Acts 1:3-12)

A sure hallmark of the new kingdom of Christ-consciousness is **detachment** from the earthly preoccupations of the False Self. As his parting admonition to the apostles, before dramatically modeling this detachment by ascending into heaven, Jesus dismisses their anxious, self-centered, "mythic membership" concern for the "kingdom of Israel"—an earthly kingdom which they *still* erroneously expected Christ to establish as a political messiah. He relativizes all such superficial, narcissistic concerns by saying, "It is not for you to know the times or seasons that the Father has established." Rather, he says, the disciples themselves—not a nationalistic or geopolitical entity—will "receive power" from the Holy Spirit to carry Christ-consciousness, not just to one nation but to "the ends of the earth." Thus it is a much **bigger** program, agenda and kingdom than the earthly nation of Israel that had been the limit of their messianic sight. The kingdom of Christ-consciousness is infinite in scope. Forget about "Israel" receiving power to dominate its neighboring countries; Jesus says, "**You** will receive power when the Holy Spirit comes upon you." The glorious spiritual evolution of Christ-consciousness that takes place in the followers of Jesus dwarfs any mere terrestrial revolution born of political ambition or the "emotional programs for happiness" of the False Self at a lower, mythic-membership level of consciousness.

The breathless, breakneck pace of the onward march of this consciousness evolution is clear as the apostles watch in stunned amazement Jesus being lifted up and away through the clouds. As they stare dumbfounded at the sky, two angelic figures appear and ask, "Why are you standing there looking at the sky? This Jesus who has been taken up from you will return in the same way as you have seen him going into heaven." There is no time to linger or dwell upon what has been taken away, but ever-more-willing and quick *relinquishment and detachment* is needed as Christ-consciousness evolves. The True Self that is yielding its ground ever more completely to the Absolute Self becomes increasingly "Teflon-like" in its detachment and "non-stick surface" that no longer clings to the earthly obsessions of the ego, but lets go instantly, knowing that nothing of value will ever be lost. Rather, all that is rapidly and willingly surrendered will be regained a hundredfold, "pressed down, shaken together, and overflowing," as Christ-consciousness returns to earth from heaven and permeates all of creation.

Suggested Prayer Intention for the 2nd Glorious Mystery:

LET ME BE in my True Self detached from all that holds me bound and tied to the bogus messianic programs of the False Self. Free me to ascend, to rise above my attachments and aversions, to live in the "heaven" of Christ-consciousness, from which I can return willingly, in freedom, to the heart of the suffering world.

(If you wish, yoke this affirmation to a positive earthly intention; now pray the second decade.)

Third Glorious Mystery: The Descent of the Holy Spirit

When the time for Pentecost was fulfilled, they were all in one place together. And suddenly there came from the sky a noise like a strong driving wind, and it filled the entire house in which they were. Then there appeared to them tongues as of fire, which parted and came to rest on each one of them. And they were all filled with the Holy Spirit and began to speak in different tongues, as the Spirit enabled them to proclaim.

Now there were devout Jews from every nation under heaven staying in Jerusalem. At this sound, they gathered in a large crowd, but they were confused because each one heard them speaking in his own language. They were astounded, and in amazement they asked, "Are not all these people who are speaking Galileans? Then how does each of us hear them in our own native language? We are Parthians, Medes, and Elamites, inhabitants of Mesopotamia, Judea and Cappadocia, Pontus and Asia, Phrygia and Pamphylia, Egypt and the districts of Libya near Cyrene, as well as travelers from Rome, both Jews and converts to Judaism, Cretans and Arabs, yet we hear them speaking in our own tongues of the mighty acts of God. They were all astounded and bewildered, and said to one another, "What does this mean?" But others said, scoffing, "They have had too much new wine." (Acts 2:1-13)

The fruit of the Spirit is love, joy, peace, patience, kindness, generosity, faithfulness, gentleness, self-control. (Galatians 5:22-23)

The Spirit, being the force of Love through which all things are created, is a universal language, the mother tongue of all creation. It "parts" and speaks individually within the depths of each human heart yet delivers a single message of unity and oneness to all, even in the midst of an ever-present diversity and multiplicity. Hence the integral "sameness" of heart among all peoples of all nations and cultures, times and tribes, despite the uniqueness and originality of each human being, unrepeatable as a snowflake or thumbprint.

The Holy Spirit is the Divine Indwelling, God-in-residence as the Absolute Self of each person. To the extent that the False Self is dismantled and the True Self (Mary) is in union with the Spirit, we live in Christ-consciousness, unity consciousness, non-dual consciousness—the "kingdom of heaven." In this heaven, every living being in its own unique incarnation shares the one core "Self" of the Self Absolute, and is divinized by the presence and action of this indwelling Holy Spirit. While we are one Spirit, one Self at core, we are "many parts," expressing the Absolute Self, the indwelling Divine Presence, in as many different tongues, dialects, lexicons, colors, shapes, sizes, and personalities as there are creatures. As we live **consciously**, in awareness of, and submission to, the Holy Spirit which is the Self Absolute, we live in love and peace with all creatures. For the Holy Spirit is the force of Love through whom all things were created. The non-dual, unity consciousness of the Risen Christ renders us madly and irrevocably in love with all creation. This is life in the Spirit.

Through baptism and chrismation with the oil that "seals" us, sacramentally, with the Holy Spirit, we can experience our own private Pentecost; however, the Holy Spirit circulates within each person and all living things, whether the sacramental system is employed or not. But it is only when we awaken in consciousness to the presence and action of the Spirit that we are truly "clothed with power from on high." It is then that we "will receive power" as Jesus promised before ascending into heaven. The sacraments of baptism and confirmation are at the service of this awakening of consciousness that enables us to access the vast power of the Holy Spirit dwelling within us, the force that empowers us to do all things through Christ, and in divine love.

As more and more people reach this level of consciousness, wars, strife, and violence will cease and the earth will become a "civilization of love." The Age of the Holy Spirit will have arrived. Until that time comes, some of those who do reach this level of "Spirit-filled" awareness will inevitably be accused of sheer lunacy, as having "had too much new wine." For those who have turned their backs on the False Self programs and mythic membership consciousness of the dominant culture are misunderstood in every generation.

Suggested Prayer Intention for the 3rd Glorious Mystery:

LET ME BE in my True Self filled with the Holy Spirit and living in conscious union with the Self Absolute. May this divine indwelling Presence guide, empower and animate all that I think, say, and do. Come, Holy Spirit, renew the face of the earth!

(If you wish, yoke this affirmation to a positive earthly intention; now pray the third decade.)

Fourth Glorious Mystery: The Assumption of Mary into Heaven

*Finally the Immaculate Virgin, preserved free from all stain of original sin, when the course of her earthly life was finished, was taken up body and soul into heavenly glory. (*Pius XII, Munificentissimus Deus, 1950*)*

*The Assumption of the Blessed Virgin is a singular participation in her Son's Resurrection and an anticipation of the resurrection of other Christians. (*Catechism of the Catholic Church, #974*)*

70

The True Self, Mary, enfleshed and bodily, is assumed into the heaven of Christ-consciousness, to live a heavenly, kingdom life. The body accompanies us into glory, just as it has been our Spirit-carrier throughout the joys, sorrows, and struggles with the False Self that have filled our earthly/spiritual journey. The mystery of the Assumption, like the Resurrection, tells us that the body can withstand the rigors of spiritual evolution and survive higher levels of consciousness than we can imagine, and that we are invited while still living this earthly life, to enter the kingdom of heaven, both **body and soul.** The body is not the exclusive domain of the False Self, as some Gnostic heresy teaches, but a faithful servant of the True Self, supporting and sustaining the breath of life while our consciousness evolves and the dross of the False Self is burned away in the purifying furnace that transforms the lead of ego into the Marian gold of divinization. With the Assumption, Mary (the True Self) completes the bridge between human and divine, earth and heaven, flesh and spirit.

Prayer Intention for the 4th Glorious Mystery:

LET ME BE in my True Self wedded faithfully to my **body** in a bond of respect and gratitude. May I be a conscious steward of the gift of this body that has provided the means for my spiritual journey.

(If you wish, yoke this affirmation to a positive earthly intention; now pray the fourth decade.)

71

Fifth Glorious Mystery: The Queenship of Mary Over Heaven and Earth

The Immaculate Virgin . . . was taken up body and soul into heavenly glory, and exalted by the Lord as Queen over all things, so that she might be the more fully conformed to her Son, the Lord of lords and conqueror of sin and death.
(Pius XII, Munificentissimus Deus, 1950)

A great sign appeared in the sky, a woman clothed with the sun, with the moon under her feet, and on her head a crown of twelve stars.
(Revelation 12:1)

The True Self is a reigning queen on the throne of personhood, for it is Mary (the True Self) who leads each person to heaven by drawing us into greater union and sublimation to the Absolute Self—Christ within—saying, "Do whatever he tells you." She is the bridge that unites body and soul, physical and spiritual, earthly and heavenly, the conditioned and the Unconditioned, time and eternity, by both dismantling the snares of the False Self and seizing the saving power of the Absolute Self during the course of our spiritual journey. In doing so, Mary, our True Self, is ever "more fully conformed to her Son," the "conqueror of sin and death." It is through her that we evolve spiritually and escape the sure death that is the wages of the sinful ego.

As the Catholic theologian Hans Urs von Balthasar wrote, "A queen enjoys full power, even with regard to the king. Mary's fullness of power is expressed in her intercession for us and her mediation of graces, so that we receive all personal graces from God." The True Self (Mary) is indeed the Mediatrix of all the graces that the Absolute Self, the indwelling Spirit of the Risen Christ, wishes to bestow, for it is only in the open mind and open heart of one who has been liberated from the False Self's tyranny that the graces of spiritual growth and transformation can be received.

Our Lady, Mary, Queen of heaven and earth, in her reign as the True Self on the throne of each person's incarnation, crushes the serpent's head of ego, overthrows the tyranny of the False Self, and gains the victory of the kingdom of heaven—Christ-consciousness—for each of us. The True Self always reigns with one foot in heaven and one foot on earth.

Suggested Prayer Intention for the 5th Glorious Mystery:

LET ME BE in my True Self always mindful of the great battle that is being waged between the False Self of my ego and the Absolute Self of God within, beckoning me to the kingdom of heaven through the intercession of my

Queen, the powerful and immaculate Blessed Virgin Mary.

(If you wish, yoke this affirmation to a positive earthly intention; now pray the fifth decade.)

Nine

From Lead to Gold: The "Magic" of the Rosary

Is contemplation of the twenty mysteries of the rosary merely an intellectual exercise? For those who never bother to read meditations or reflections on them, do they facilitate spiritual growth at all? Or is mere rote repetition of the bead prayers all that is accomplished?

In Medjugorje, inexplicably, the actual *physical material* of the rosary changes in appearance, the chain turning from a leaden gray or silver color to gold. What does it mean? Some speculate that such supernatural occurrences signal a special blessing, being favored by God or by Mary. Some become entranced by the phenomenon itself, turn into "Medj-heads," and buy tons of Medjugorje rosaries, setting about to pray on them, pass them to friends and relatives, and watch them intently for color change, "seeking a sign" as Jesus said. One does not need to look far to find amazing, spectacular true-life stories—spanning the pages of history from medieval times to the present—of illnesses cured, lives saved, marriages salvaged, rescues accomplished, heroic feats achieved, and battles won through the rosary. Sometimes the prayer was fervent; sometimes the literal string of beads itself saved the day. Testimonies abound. Thus many whose rosaries change color in Medjugorje dream of an even more spectacular punchline to follow.

But perhaps a simpler, more literal reading of the miracle is better. After all, what is actually happening? **Change.** Perhaps the medium is the message, and this is all we need to glean from it: a dawning realization that if something as "impossible" as a rosary physically transforming from lead to gold before our eyes can happen, then maybe—just maybe—"I" could change, too. Maybe the leaden grayness of soul that is "me" could be transformed, converted, transmuted, and evolve into the gold of divinization. But how? Again, we may need only open our eyes to what is before us: a string of beads designed to be prayed on.

The Importance of an Inner Observer or Witnessing Presence

Throughout the ages and across the many traditions, teachers of the spiritual life have known and taught that the spiritual journey of shifting from the level of consciousness in which the False Self is in charge to one in which the True Self reigns necessitates a stable "witnessing" presence or **inner observer** who keeps track of the "big picture" and mediates between these two very different levels of consciousness. This mediating presence is necessary for the transmutation of "lead" into "gold," that is, the transformation of a False Self-dominated consciousness into unitive, transcendent, Christ-consciousness. This "witness" or mediating presence does not identify with any egoic programs, but watches one's life from a deeper core or center of gravity than the egoic level; it watches from the profound level of **Being** rather than the "doing" or "action" level of life.

The inner observer serves to connect the two worlds within—the ego world and the Divine world—to establish communication and bring them together at the "crossroads" or intersection that is the True Self: "Mary" who joins heaven and earth, God and humanity, in her very being. The witness is able to look with compassion at both the deeply personal, individualistic, egoic lower self, and the higher, transpersonal Self, and seeks a marriage of the two, a wedding feast. The primary function of the inner observer or witnessing presence is as a link, a bridge or connector that unites all parts of the self in awareness, in unconditional presence to Reality, so that one can fully inhabit one's being, and experience the force and energy of Spirit—God—flowing through and driving all things.

Mirroring the homeostasis of the universe, at the core of self, Being remains calmly stable despite everything that might be happening, emotionally, on the surface of life. The egoic mind alone cannot sustain this sense of stability or inner peace; only the inner witness or observer (the True Self/Mary) can do it. This True Self is the integral point of one's being, the magnetic center. The True Self is at home in God, no matter what the exterior circumstances or situation, residing in a state of equilibrium, balanced and centered—neither "hopped up" at the extreme of blissful ecstasy nor drowning in the extreme of abject sorrow.

The rosary is an ideal tool for facilitating the engagement of the Witness or Inner Observer. Throughout the prayer practice of saying the rosary, one is observing, impartially, the events of the life of Jesus and Mary. Dispassionately and compassionately, we lay a prayer—the Hail Mary—alongside each event. The mantric, drone-like rhythm of the prayer prevents us from becoming identified with the egoic drama of the mysteries. Continuously we invoke the higher state of consciousness that is the True Self, Mary, to pray for us in our lower, egoic state, now and at the hour of death which must come for all that is false. What is True will never die.

We pray through mysteries of life and Being that are joyful, sorrowful, luminous and glorious, maintaining an emotional equanimity and steady peace amidst them all. This is precisely what spiritual evolution moves toward: a disinterested love for all that is, without discrimination, conditions or resistance.

A Bridge between Body and Spirit

As bridge between the bodily, physical, material reality that is the only domain the ego knows, and the higher consciousness that is accessible through silence, meditation, and prayer, the rosary is an unparalleled tool. The beads on a chain keep our body engaged and participating, and we remain grounded in our incarnate reality, tied to the earth through the sense of touch and physical motor skills demanded to move from one bead to the next, one prayer to the next, one mystery to the next. We stay connected to the physical world represented in the metal, string, leather, or woolen knots, the stone, wood, glass, or shell beads. Simultaneously, we allow our spirit to transcend the earth-bound dimension as we enter into the meditative state that the repeated sacred words of Scripture facilitate. The rosary is eminently *incarnational* and thus ideal for manifesting the True Self/Mary. It accomplishes this through the subtle yet sure development of the Inner Observer or Witnessing Presence that is indispensable for spiritual evolution, for the transformation of the "lead" of our False Self into the "gold" of Christ-consciousness.

A Spiral Staircase of Evolutionary Mysteries

Will this transformative process be linear and straight? Usually not. Rather, the rosary acts upon our spiritual evolution more in the form of a *spiral staircase.* With each progressive step we take upward there is a concurrent lateral movement that preserves the insights we gained at a lower level, so that the unfolding mysteries of the rosary, in perfect imitation of life and consciousness evolution, both *transcend and include* every previous level. We revisit familiar territory, but from a higher vantage point, occasionally falling back a step, yet moving steadily upward as the insights of the Glorious mysteries build upon the Luminous, the Luminous upon the Sorrowful, the Sorrowful upon the Joyful, with none of them forgotten or abandoned. Hence in this deeply integral journey, we pray all of the mysteries at various times, accepting everything, leaving no part of the evolutionary truth behind.

Part of the deep mystical wisdom of the rosary is that it is structured upon the "Life Conditions" of Jesus and Mary; all evolution occurs in response to the demands of *changing life conditions* which necessitate a movement up the spiral, to the next step. The crisis, stress or wake-up call that pushes evolution may take the form of a pregnancy, travel, profound encounter with another, religious rite of passage, or the sheer panic of loss (Joyful Mysteries); it may take the form of mental, emotional, and spiritual anguish or aridity, emptiness, persecution, or severe physical diminishment (Sorrowful Mysteries); it may take the form of falling in love, ecstatic joy, intellectual accomplishment, enlightenment, supernatural peak experiences, or mystical experience (Luminous Mysteries). We are all immersed in ever-changing life conditions, some of which spur us out of our comfort zone to evolutionary movement. The rosary takes us on a journey of recapitulating the Christ-life as our own, experiencing it from the vantage point of the witnessing presence of our True Self (Mary). Thus it is a timeless tool that is perpetually timely.

Ten

From Personal to Global Change through the Rosary

"Precisely because Mary is with God and in God, she is very close to each one of us. While she lived on this earth she could only be close to a few people. Being in God, who is actually 'within' all of us, Mary shares in this closeness of God." —Pope Benedict XVI

If God is within all of us, and Mary is "in God," then, by clear deductive reasoning, Mary is in all of us, too. Again and again, in the Medjugorje messages, Mary says, "I am with you and I intercede before God for each of you." The True Self intercedes and mediates between the ego and the Self Absolute or Divine Indwelling presence of God. It is the True Self (Mary) who is able, as a witnessing presence, to relativize, moderate, order, and discern the myriad supplications of the False Self, its frantic pleas for safety and security, affection and esteem, power and control. The True Self sifts, in a sieve-like fashion, the intentions arising from both ego and from higher consciousness, separating wheat from chaff before presenting to the Absolute Self, the Divine Indwelling, what is needed for change—the "chain links" of the self that require a spiritual alchemy to take them from silvery lead to gold. Scripture says, "Our God is a consuming fire." (*Heb.*

12:29; Deut 4:24) Indeed, once the petition for change is submitted to the burning furnace of transformation by Mary (the True Self), *prayer is answered.*

The quality of our consciousness determines the quality of our thoughts and the force of their magnetic power to attract concrete change into physical manifestation. Because the rosary is designed to be entirely at the service of the evolution of consciousness or spiritual transformation at the deepest levels, it is one of the most powerful weapons that exist in the arsenal of spiritual technologies. It is the spiritual equivalent of a *nuclear power plant,* having unimaginable potential to effect massive change on our planet through the annihilation of the egocentric consciousness that currently dominates world cultures. Until the ego or False Self is mastered and subdued in human consciousness, kept firmly and squarely beneath the "heel" of Mary (the True Self), the Big Problems of our planet, such as global environmental destruction, war, poverty and hunger, the AIDS epidemic, genocide, and all socio-economic injustice, will remain to threaten our very extinction. There is little that we can do, individually, that will have greater impact on these "Big Problems" of our time than to *pray the rosary.* The greater our awareness, wakefulness, and consciousness of the Witnessing Presence as we tell the beads, the more profound will be the impact of our prayer.

In Medjugorje, Mary said, "With prayer, wars can be stopped. . . . With prayer, even the laws of nature can be suspended." Indeed, this is evident in that small corner of Bosnia-Hercegovina, from natural elements such as sun, stars, fire, flora, air and metal behaving in spectacularly supernatural ways, to bitter enmity in the hearts of pilgrims melting into forgiveness and compassion, to normal physical processes such as the need to eat, drink, sleep, and eliminate being strangely suspended, to the radical reversal of incurable diseases, to the fact that even at the height of the Serbo-Croatian war, Medjugorje was untouched by bombs aimed at it, despite the best efforts of air force bombers overhead, who were unable to strike due to sudden cloud cover that always shrouded their target even on the clearest of sunny days. Medjugorje's bomb-and-bullet-proof cloak was the *rosary,* prayed intentionally and incessantly by all the villagers and pilgrims.

Its effects will be no less dramatic in the life of anyone who takes hold of this prayer form for the cause of conversion of heart, as Our Lady, Queen of Peace, the True Self, asks. *The change is the thing.* The imperative of evolutionary change, embodied in every mystery of the rosary consciously prayed, is the antidote needed for any situation about which we intercede, whether personal, interpersonal, transpersonal, or planetary. As our consciousness level rises, the scope of our intentions becomes broader, moving from concerns that are **egocentric** ("my issues"), to **ethnocentric** ("my group's" issues), to *worldcentric* (all human issues), to **eco-centric** (the whole earth's issues), to **cosmocentric** (the good of All that Is). Finding its level in each person who prays, Mary's rosary is ever a force for personal and global transformation.

Rosary for Planet Earth, Our Home

Bring the power of your conscious intention to these or other intercessions for our world!

Joyful Mysteries: 1) For our Biosphere; 2) For our Vegetation/Plant life; 3) For our Oceans and all Sea Creatures; 4) For Animals & Other Creatures—20,000 species per year going extinct; 5) For Hungry Humans and Those without Basic Survival Necessities, that all may be fed.

Sorrowful Mysteries: 1) For Religious Tolerance and Mutual Respect among Religions; 2) For Racial Equality and Mutual Respect among Races; 3) For Gender Equality and Mutual Respect between the Sexes; 4) For Sexual Orientation Equality and Mutual Respect between Heterosexual and Homosexual Persons; 5) For Peace among All Nations with Tolerance for Diverse Political and Socio-economic Systems.

Luminous Mysteries: 1) For The Development of Alternative Energy Sources (solar, wind, etc.); 2) For an End to Waste and Overconsumption of the Earth's Goods; 3) For Conservation of Electricity and Water; 4) For Conscious Eating and Food Choices; 5) For Conservation of Fossil Fuels (by walking, cycling, mass transit, hybrid vehicles, etc.).

Glorious Mysteries: 1) That Natural Disasters Might be Averted or Lessened in Effect; 2) That Accidents Causing Harm might be Averted or Lessened in Effect: 3) That Health Crises might be Averted or Lessened in Effect; 4) For Reconciliation in Marriages and Families; 5) For Healing of Addictions in all forms.

Appendix I: Prayers of the Rosary

Before beginning the "bead" prayers of the Rosary, one starts by holding the crucifix and reciting **the Apostle's Creed:**

I believe in God, the Father almighty,
Maker of heaven and earth,
And I believe in Jesus Christ, his only Son, our Lord,
Who was conceived by the Holy Spirit,
born of the Virgin Mary, suffered under Pontius Pilate,
was crucified, died, and was buried.
He descended into hell. On the third day he rose again.
He ascended into heaven and is seated at the right hand
    of the Father;
from thence he shall come to judge the living and the
    dead.
I believe in the Holy Spirit, the holy Catholic Church,
The communion of saints, the forgiveness of sins,
the resurrection of the body, and the life everlasting.
    Amen.

*(In Medjugorje, Mary has stated that the Apostle's Creed is the prayer she most enjoys hearing. At the very start of the rosary, we are setting out our belief and firm conviction that we have a **Source** and a **Spirit** through which we are united to that Source in oneness with all creation.*

This belief is the basis from which we are empowered to pray, evolve, and manifest God in our lives.)

On the single, or larger, beads of the Rosary, one prays the "**Our Father**" (or Lord's Prayer):

Our Father, who art in heaven, hallowed be thy name.
Thy kingdom come, thy will be done, on earth as it is in
    heaven.
Give us this day our daily bread, and forgive us our
    trespasses,
As we forgive those who trespass against us.
And lead us not into temptation, but deliver us from
    evil.

On the smaller beads in decades (groups of ten), one prays the "**Hail Mary**":

Hail Mary, full of grace! The Lord is with you.
Blessed are you among women,
and blessed is the fruit of your womb, Jesus.
Holy Mary, Mother of God, pray for us sinners now
and at the hour of our death. Amen.

At the end of each decade, one prays the "**Glory Be**" (or Gloria):

Glory be to the Father, and to the Son, and to the Holy
    Spirit,
as it was in the beginning, is now, and ever shall be,
world without end. Amen.

Upon completion of the Rosary, one prays the "**Hail, Holy Queen**" (or Salve Regina):

Hail, Holy Queen, Mother of mercy,
Our life, our sweetness, and our hope.
To thee do we cry, poor banished children of Eve,
To thee do we lift up our sighs, mourning and weeping in this valley of tears.
Turn then, O most gracious Advocate, thine eyes of mercy toward us, and after this, our exile,
Show unto us the blessed fruit of thy womb, Jesus.
O clement, O loving, O sweet Virgin Mary!
Pray for us, O holy Mother of God,
that we may be made worthy of the promises of Christ.

Appendix II

Summary of Prayer Intentions for Each Mystery

	Joyful	Sorrowful	Luminous	Glorious
1	**Annunciation** Virginal openness of mind and heart; saying Yes to God in total commitment of love	**Agony in the Garden** Wakefulness and awareness; yielding in will to the necessity of transformative suffering	**Baptism of Jesus** Infusion of Holy Spirit conviction that one is Beloved of God; eagerness to confront demons of False Self	**Resurrection** Consciousness of infinite possibility beyond the tomb of egoic fears and needs
2	**Visitation** Urgency to aid others toward God consciousness; magnifying God at all times	**Scourging** Benefiting in the True Self from the humiliation of ego that comes with physical diminishment	**Wedding at Cana** Sensitive awareness of need and power to respond promptly in the moment	**Ascension** Detachment from False Self messianic claims, returning to heart of suffering world in freedom from egoism
3	**Birth of Jesus** Humility, simplicity, and voluntary poverty as transparency needed for the True Self to manifest	**Crowning with Thorns** Liberation from negative, afflictive, destructive thoughts through prayer at one's center/heart	**Proclamation of Kingdom** Continual repentance, change, conversion, transformation from ego-centric to Christocentric life	**Descent of Holy Spirit** Empowerment and animation of the Indwelling Divinity in all that one thinks and does
4	**Presentation in Temple** Spiritual context and practice as part of a community	**Carrying the Cross** Taking responsibility for situations created by False Self; intentionally laying down that life	**Transfiguration** Glorious revelation of Divine Indwelling through silent listening prayer that manifests God	**Assumption of Mary** The manifestation of the True Self through a body respected and cared for
5	**Finding in the Temple** Expanding one's sphere of concern beyond "me" to "we" consciousness	**Crucifixion** Courageous passage through the Dark Night, abiding in True Self as ego is put to death	**Last Supper/Eucharist** Unity consciousness: recognizing essential oneness of all creation with God	**Queenship of Mary** Mindfulness of the great battle between False Self and Absolute Self waged through the intercession of Mary, the True Self

Appendix III: A Rosary Mandala

A mandala (from the Sanskrit word for *"circle"*) is a cosmic diagram in a circular pattern that symbolically depicts the organizational structure of life in its wholeness or completion. It is used in various spiritual traditions as a meditation aid, for focusing one's attention and helping to access deeper levels of the unconscious and a mystical sense of oneness with the core unity from which all forms arise. While used primarily in Hindu and Buddhist practice, examples of Christian mandalas include the labyrinth in the Chartres Cathedral, the Celtic cross, and stained glass rose windows. The following is a new form of Christian mandala: a **Rosary Mysteries Mandala.**

Appendix IV: Medjugorje Messages

Below is a brief compendium of Mary's words to the visionaries of Medjugorje on the relevant topics of this book.

On Conversion of Heart or Transformation of Consciousness:

"Today I invite you to conversion. This is the most important message that I have given you here." (2/25/96)

"Today again I am calling you to complete conversion, which is difficult for those who have not chosen God." (1/25/88)

"God blesses you day after day and desires a change of your life. Therefore, pray that you may have the strength to change your life." (5/25/90)

"I invite you to life and to change all the negative in you, so that it all turns into the positive and live." (5/25/91)

"I invite you to change your life because you have taken a path of misery, a path of ruin. When I told you: convert, pray, fast, be reconciled, you took these messages superficially." (4/25/92)

"I love you and that is why I am with you, in order to teach you and to lead you to a new life of conversion and renunciation. Only in this way will you discover God and all that which now seems so far away from you." (11/25/92)

"I wish that each of you decide for a change of life. . . . You cannot say that you are converted, because your life must become a daily conversion. In order to understand what you have to do, little children, pray and God will give you what you have to do, and where you have to change." (2/25/93)

"Rejoice because God loves you and gives you the possibility to convert every day and to believe more in God the Creator." (5/25/94)

"Today I invite you to prayer because only in prayer can you understand my coming here. The Holy Spirit will enlighten you to understand that you must convert. . . . You do not accept the way of conversion, the way of salvation that I am offering you through these apparitions. Little children, pray, convert your hearts and come closer to me. May good overcome evil." (7/25/95)

"When God is in the first place, then you will, in all that you do, seek the will of God. In this way your daily conversion will become easier. Seek with humility that which is not in order in your hearts, and you shall understand what you have to do. Conversion will become a daily duty that you will do with joy. . . . I invite you to become my witness by prayer and personal conversion." (4/25/96)

"Pray in order to understand that you all, through your

life and your example, ought to collaborate in the work of salvation. I wish that all people convert and see me and my Son, Jesus, in you. I will intercede for you and help you to become the light." (5/25/96)

"Decide for conversion, that your life may be true before God, so that in the truth of your life you witness the beauty God gave you. ... Decide for prayer because through prayer, you will be able to live the conversion." (7/25/96)

"Today I invite you to open yourselves to God the Creator, so that He changes you. ... I wish to renew you and lead you with my Heart to the Heart of Jesus, which still today suffers for you and calls you to conversion and renewal. Through you, I wish to renew the world. Comprehend, little children, that you are today the salt of the earth and the light of the world. I invite you and I love you and in a special way implore: Convert!" (10/25/96)

"Decide for God the Creator. Allow Him to transform and change you." (5/25/98)

"In the silence of the heart, remain with Jesus, so that He may change and transform you with His love." (7/25/98)

"Today I call you to open yourselves completely to me so that I may transform you and lead you to the heart of my son Jesus." (10/25/98)

"Open your hearts and give me everything that is in them ... that I may offer them to Jesus; so that with His immeasurable love, He may burn and transform your sorrows into the joy of His resurrection." (2/25/99)

"Also today I call you to conversion. You are concerned too much about material things and little about spiritual ones. Open your hearts and start again to work more on your personal conversion." (4/25/00)

"Pray, pray, pray for the conversion of your heart, so that Jesus may be born in you all and may dwell in you and come to reign over your entire being." (12/25/01)

"You are still attached to earthly things and little to spiritual life. . . . Decide for God and for daily conversion. You cannot be converted, little children, if you do not abandon sins and do not decide for love towards God and neighbor." (1/25/02)

"Open yourselves to prayer and seek a conversion of your hearts from God." (5/25/02)

"Decide also today for God, that in you and through you He may change the hearts of people, and also your hearts." (4/25/03)

"I call all of you to conversion. If you convert, all those around you will also be renewed and prayer will be a joy for them." (5/25/03)

"Pray in a special way for all those who have not come to know God's love. Pray that their hearts may open and draw closer to my heart and the Heart of my son Jesus, so that we can transform them into people of peace and love." (1/25/04)

"Pray and rejoice with me for every heart that has converted and become an instrument of peace in the world." (6/25/04)

"Decide, as in the first days of my coming here, for a complete change of your life." (8/25/04)

"I feel pain for each one who is far from my heart; but I do not leave you alone. I believe you can leave the way of sin and decide for holiness." (9/25/05)

"I call you to conversion. Children, through all this time which God permitted me to be with you, I continuously called you to conversion. Many of your hearts remained closed. . . . Pray to [Jesus] for the gift of conversion." (12/25/05)

On Each Person's Responsibility to Evolve in Consciousness:

"I do not wish to force anyone to do that which he/she neither feels nor desires." (4/30/84)

"Begin to work in your hearts as you are working in the fields. Work and change your hearts so that a new spirit from God can take its place in your hearts." (4/25/85)

"Today I call you to start working on your own hearts." (10/17/85)

"Dear children, do not allow Satan to get control of your hearts, so you would be an image of Satan and not of me. I call you to pray for how you might be a witness of my presence. Without you, God cannot bring to reality that which

He desires. God has given a free will to everyone, and it's in your control." (1/30/86)

"I call you to give your heart so I can change it to be like mine. . . . You are not able [to respond] because you have not given me your heart so I can change it." (5/15/86)

"These years I have been calling you to pray, to live what I am telling you, but you are living my messages a little. You talk, but do not live; that is why, little children, this war is lasting so long. . . . Dear children, I cannot help you if you do not live God's commandments, if you do not live the Mass, if you do not give up sin. I invite you to be apostles of love and goodness. In this world of unrest give witness to God and God's love." (10/25/93)

"Wake up from the sleep of unbelief and sin, because this is a time of grace which God gives you." (2/25/00)

"Awaken from the tired sleep of your soul and say yes to God with all your strength. I am with you, little children, and I call you to perfection of your soul and of everything you do." (3/25/01)

"Do not delay, but say with all your heart: 'I want to help Jesus and Mary that all the more brothers and sisters may come to know the way of holiness.' " (10/25/03)

"Be those who draw souls to God and not those who distance them." (2/25/04)

"I call you to be love where there is hatred and food where there is hunger. Open your hearts, little children, and let your hands be extended and generous so that, through

you, every creature may thank God the Creator."
(9/25/04)

"Be courageous witnesses of Good News in every situation." (12/25/04)

"I call you to interior renunciation. The way to this leads you through love, fasting, prayer and good works. Only with total interior renunciation will you recognize God's love and the signs of the time in which you live." (3/18/06)

On the Power of the Rosary:

"I would like the people to pray along with me these days. And to pray as much as possible! And to fast on Wednesdays and Fridays, and every day to pray at least one Rosary; the joyful, sorrowful and glorious mysteries." (8/14/84)
(This was before the Luminous Mysteries of the Rosary were added by Pope John Paul II.)

"Call on everyone to pray the Rosary. With the rosary you shall overcome all the adversities which Satan is trying to inflict. . . . Dedicate your time to the Rosary!" (7/25/85)

"I call you especially now to advance against Satan by means of prayer. Dear children, put on the armor for battle and with the Rosary in your hand defeat him!" (8/8/85)

"Today I call you to begin to pray the Rosary with a living faith. . . . I am calling you to pray the Rosary and that your Rosary be an obligation which you shall fulfill with joy. . . . You shall understand the reason I am with you this long. I desire to teach you to pray." (6/12/86)

"Pray and let the Rosary always be in your hand as a sign to Satan that you belong to me." (2/25/88)

"If you so wish, grasp for the Rosary. Even the Rosary alone can work miracles in the world and in your lives." (1/25/91)

"I call all priests and religious brothers and sisters to pray the Rosary and to teach others to pray. The rosary, little children, is especially dear to me. Through the rosary open your heart to me and I am able to help you." (8/25/97)

"Little children, prayer works miracles. When you are tired and sick and you do not know the meaning of your life, take the Rosary and pray; pray until prayer becomes for you a joyful meeting with your Savior." (4/25/01)

On the Struggle Against the Ego or False Self:

"I will pray my son Jesus to give you the grace to experience the victory of Jesus in the temptations of Satan." (7/12/84)

"Satan is so strong and with all his might wants to disturb my plans which I have begun with you. You pray, just pray and don't stop for a minute! . . . And don't let Satan discourage you. He is working hard in the world. Be on your guard!" (1/14/85)

"Dear children, Satan is lurking for each individual. Especially in everyday affairs he wants to spread confusion among each one of you. Therefore, my call to you is that your day would be only prayer and complete surrender to God." (9/4/86)

"By your prayer and your life you help to destroy everything that is evil in people and uncover the deception that Satan makes use of. You pray that the truth prevails in all hearts." (9/25/86)

"I am calling you to prayer and complete surrender to God, because Satan wants to sift you through everyday affairs and in your life he wants to snatch the first place. Therefore, pray without ceasing!" (10/16/86)

"You pray, dear children! Only that way shall you be able to recognize all the evil that is in you and surrender it to the Lord so the Lord may completely purify your hearts." (12/4/86)

"Dear children, you are ready to commit sin, and to put yourselves in the hand of Satan without reflecting. I call on each one of you to consciously decide for God and against Satan." (5/25/87)

"I desire that your decisions be free before God, because He has given you freedom. Therefore, pray, so that, free from any influence of Satan, we may decide only for God." (11/25/89)

"Pray and do not permit Satan to work in your life through misunderstandings, the nonunderstanding and nonacceptance of one another." (1/25/90)

"I want you to renounce all the things to which you are attached but which are hurting your spiritual life. . . . Decide completely for God and do not allow Satan to come into your life through those things that hurt both you and your spiritual life." (2/25/90)

"I am with you even if you are not conscious of it. I want to protect you from everything that Satan offers you and through which he wants to destroy you." (3/25/90)

"Today, like never before, I invite you to prayer. . . . Satan is strong and desires to destroy not only human life, but also nature and the planet on which you live." (1/25/91)

"Now as never before Satan wants to show the world his shameful face by which he wants to seduce as many people as possible onto the way of death and sin. . . . Forget your desires, dear children, and pray for what God desires, and not for what you desire." (9/25/91)

"These days are the days when you need to decide for God, for peace and for the good. May every hatred and jealousy disappear from your life and your thoughts, and may there only dwell love for God and for your neighbor. . . . I guide you into a new time." (1/25/93)

"Satan wants war, wants lack of peace, wants to destroy all which is good. Therefore, dear children, pray, pray, pray." (3/25/93)

"I am with you to love and protect you; to protect your hearts from Satan and to bring you all closer to the heart of my Son, Jesus." (6/25/93)

"I want your life to be bound to me. I am your Mother, and I do not want Satan to deceive you for he wants to lead you the wrong way, but he cannot if you do not let him." (7/25/93)

"In these times Satan wants to create disorder in your hearts and in your families. Little children, do not give in. You should not allow him to lead you and your life." (1/25/94)

"Satan is tempting you, and in the smallest thing, your faith disappears. This is why, little children, pray and through prayer, you will have blessing and peace." (3/25/95)

"Do not permit Satan to pull you apart and do with you what he wants." (1/25/98)

"Do not forget that you are here on earth on the way to eternity and that your home is in Heaven. That is why, little children, be open to God's love and leave *egoism* and sin." (7/25/00)

On Love:

"I, the Mother, love you all. And in any moment that is difficult for you, do not be afraid! Because I love you even when you are far from me and my son." (5/24/84)

"No, you don't know how to love and you don't know how to listen with love to the words I am saying to you. Be conscious, my beloved, that I am your Mother and I have come on earth to teach you to listen out of love, to pray out of love, and not compelled by the fact that you are carrying a cross. By means of the cross God is glorified through every person." (11/29/84)

"Dear children, through love you will achieve everything and even what you think is impossible." (2/28/85)

"I am calling you to love of neighbor and love toward the one from whom evil comes to you. In that way with love you will be able to discern the intentions of hearts. Pray and love, dear children! By love you are able to do even that which you think is impossible." (11/17/85)

"The more you will to love your neighbor, the more you shall experience Jesus." (12/19/85)

"I wish to lead you further in love. Abandon your hearts to me!" (12/26/85)

"I invite you to the greatest sacrifice, the sacrifice of love. Without love, you are not able to accept either me or my Son. Without love, you cannot give an account of your experiences to others. Therefore, dear children, I call you to begin to live love within yourselves." (3/27/86)

"You do not know, dear children, how great my love is, and you do not know how to accept it. In various ways I wish to show it to you but you do not recognize it. You do not understand my words with your heart and neither are you able to comprehend my love. Dear children, accept me in your life and so you will be able to accept all I am saying to you and to which I am calling you." (5/22/86)

"Without love, dear children, you can do nothing. . . . I am calling you to live in mutual love. . . . start loving from today with an ardent love, the love with which I love you." (5/29/86)

"With love overcome every sin and with love overcome all the difficulties which are coming to you. Dear children, I beseech you to live love within yourselves." (7/10/86)

"Let your only instrument always be love. By love turn everything into good which Satan desires to destroy and possess. Only that way shall you be completely mine and I shall be able to help you." (7/31/86)

"Pray, because in prayer each one of you will be able to achieve complete love." (10/25/87)

"Pray that you might be able to comprehend what God desires to tell you through my presence and through the messages I am giving you. . . . Pray that from your heart would flow a fountain of love to every person, both to the one who hates you and to the one who despises you. That way you will be able through Jesus' love to overcome all the misery in this world of sorrows." (11/25/91)

"May your life become a continuous prayer. Without love you cannot pray." (11/25/92)

"Today I call you to love. Without love, you can neither live with God nor with brother. Therefore, I call all of you to open your hearts to the love of God that is so great and open to each one of you. . . . If you do not first love God, then you will neither be able to love neighbor nor the one you hate. Therefore, little children, pray and through prayer you will discover love." (4/25/95)

"God is great and His love for every creature is great. Therefore, pray to be able to understand the love and goodness of God." (10/25/95)

"I desire that you become apostles of love. By loving, little children, it will be recognized that you are mine." (3/25/98)

"I desire for my Jesus' heart and your heart to become one heart of love and peace. . . . Jesus is the way of love." (7/25/99)

"Peacelessness has begun to reign in hearts and hatred reigns in the world. That is why, you who live my messages be the light and extended hands to this faithless world that all may come to know the God of Love." (11/25/01)

"Pray, little children, for unity of Christians, that all may be one heart. Unity will really be among you inasmuch as you will pray and forgive. Do not forget: love will conquer only if you pray, and your heart will open." (1/25/05)

"By prayer and your love, the world will set out on a better way and love will begin to rule the world." (4/25/05)

On the Power of Prayer for Evolving One's Level of Consciousness:

"Pray, and you shall not regret it. God will give you gifts by which you will glorify Him till the end of your life on this earth." (6/2/84)

"Pray, pray, pray!" (6/21/84)

"Without prayer there is no peace." (9/6/84)

"You are not conscious of the messages which God is sending you through me. He is giving you great graces and you do not comprehend them. Pray to the Holy Spirit for enlightenment. If you only knew how great are the graces God is granting you, you would be praying without ceasing." (11/8/94)

"You are not conscious of every message I am giving you. Now I just want to say—pray, pray, pray! I don't know what else to tell you because I love you and I want you to comprehend my love and God's love through prayer." (11/15/84)

"Pray, pray, pray! In prayer you shall perceive the greatest joy and the way out of every situation that has no exit." (3/28/85)

"I call you again to prayer with the heart. Let prayer be your everyday food. . . . Pray, and then you shall overcome even every weariness. Prayer will be your joy and your rest." (5/30/85)

"I beseech you, dear children, come to prayer with awareness. In prayer you shall come to know the greatness of God." (11/28/85)

"Without prayer, dear children, you are not able to experience either God, or me or the graces which I am giving you." (7/3/86)

"You, dear children, are not able to understand how great the value of prayer is as long as you yourself do not say: 'Now is the time for prayer, now nothing else is important to me, now not one person is important to me but God.'" (10/2/86)

"I am calling you to pray with your whole heart and day by day to change your life." (11/13/86)

"You cannot open yourselves to God if you do not pray. Therefore, from today, decide to consecrate a time in the day only for an encounter with God in silence." (7/25/89)

"Pray, pray, pray! Let prayer begin to rule in the whole world." (8/25/89)

"Let each of you find time for prayer so that in prayer you discover God. I do not desire you to talk about prayer, but to pray. Let your every day be filled with prayer of gratitude to God for life and for all that you have. I do not desire your life to pass by in words but that you glorify God with deeds." (4/25/91)

"If you pray, God will help you to discover the true reason for my coming. . . . Pray and read the sacred Scriptures so that through my coming you discover the messages in sacred Scripture for you." (6/25/91)

"I desire you to grasp the seriousness of the situation and that much of what will happen depends on your prayers and you are praying a little bit. Dear children, I am with you and I am inviting you to begin to pray and fast seriously as in the first days of my coming." (7/25/91)

"Only by prayer and fasting can war be stopped. . . . Accept the call to prayer with seriousness." (4/25/92)

"Please accept my call and start to pray in a new way until prayer becomes joy to you. Then you will discover that God is all powerful in your daily life." (5/25/92)

"Pray, pray, pray, because prayer is the foundation of your peace." (6/25/97)

"Through a personal experience of prayer you may be able to discover the beauty of God's creatures. You cannot speak or witness about prayer, if you do not pray. That is why, little children, in the silence of the heart, remain with Jesus, so that He may change and transform you with His love." (7/25/98)

"Little children, the one who prays is not afraid of the future and the one who fasts is not afraid of evil. Once again, I repeat to you: only through prayer and fasting also wars can be stopped—wars of your unbelief and fear for the future." (1/25/01)

"You do not be afraid because the one who prays is not afraid of evil and has no hatred in the heart." (9/25/01)

"Through you and your prayer, peace will begin to flow

through the world. . . . pray, pray, pray, because prayer works miracles in human hearts and in the world. I am with you and I thank God for each of you who has accepted and lives prayer with seriousness." (10/25/01)

"Also today I call you to prayer. Little children, believe that by simple prayer miracles can be worked. . . . God gives you graces and you do not see them. Pray and you will see them. May your day be filled with prayer and thanksgiving for everything that God gives you." (10/25/02)

"Again, I call you to pray, pray, pray, not with words but with the heart." (12/25/02)

"Pray, and in prayer you are open to God's will; in this way, in everything you do, you realize God's plan in you and through you." (3/25/03)